W9-CDC-498

OLD INNS OF ENGLAND IN COLOUR

OLD INNS OF ENGLAND
IN COLOUR

A Collection of Colour Photographs

With an Introductory Text and Notes on the Illustrations by

WILLIAM GAUNT

LONDON
B. T. BATSFORD LTD

First published, 1958

PRINTED AND BOUND IN GREAT BRITAIN
BY JARROLD AND SONS LTD, LONDON AND NORWICH
FOR THE PUBLISHERS
B. T. BATSFORD LTD.
4 FITZHARDINGE STREET, PORTMAN SQUARE, LONDON, W.1

CONTENTS

LIST OF ILLUSTRATIONS

LIST OF ILLUSTRATIONS

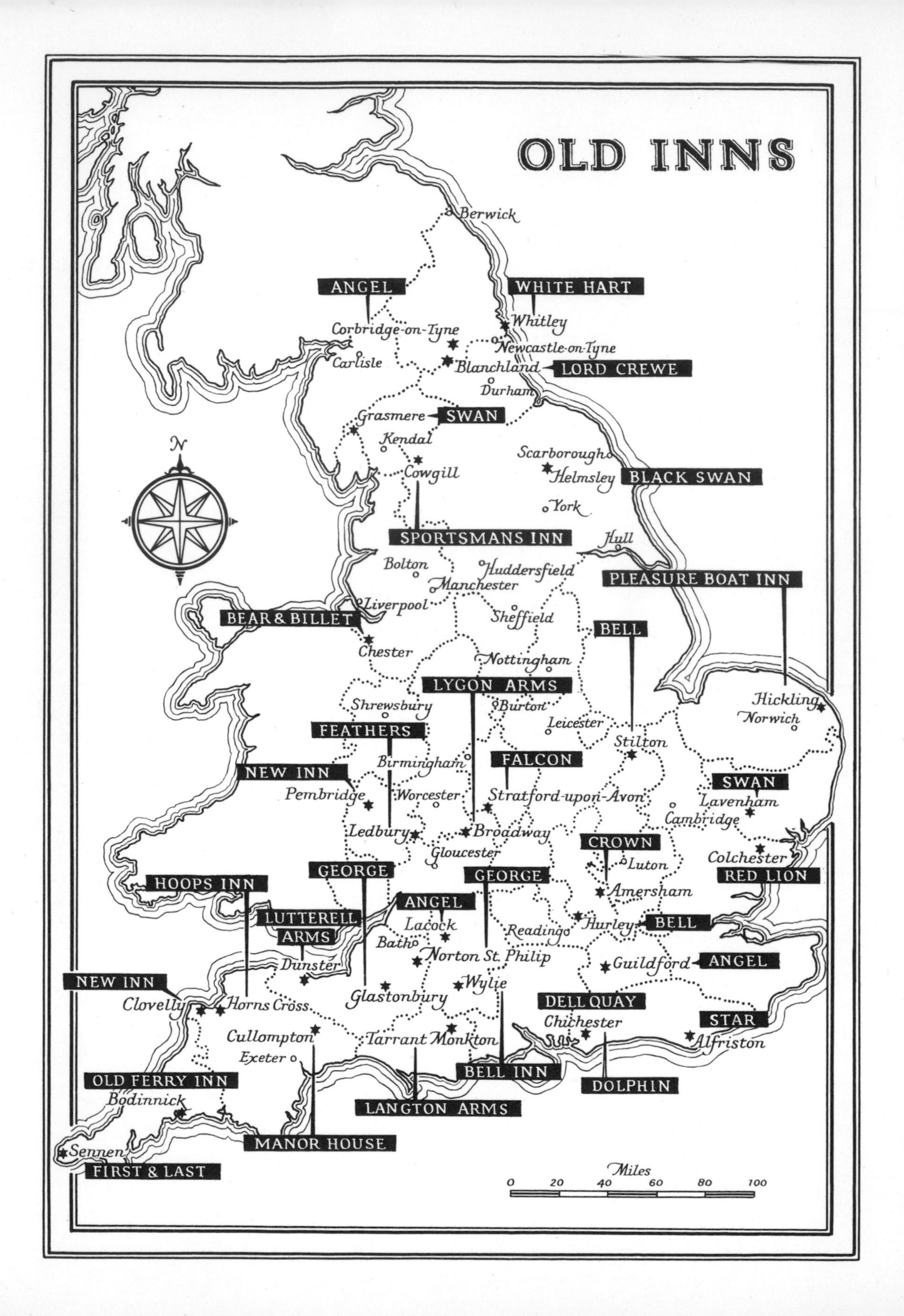
OLD INNS
Berwick
ANGEL
WHITE HART
Whitley
Corbridge-on-Tyne
Newcastle-on-Tyne
Carlisle
Blanchland
LORD CREWE
Durham
Grasmere
SWAN
Kendal
Cowgill
Scarborough
Helmsley
BLACK SWAN
York
SPORTSMANS INN
Hull
Bolton
Huddersfield
Manchester
PLEASURE BOAT INN
Liverpool
BEAR & BILLET
Sheffield
BELL
Chester
Nottingham
LYGON ARMS
Burton
Shrewsbury
Hickling
Norwich
FEATHERS
Leicester
Stilton
Birmingham
FALCON
NEW INN
SWAN
Pembridge
Worcester
Stratford-upon-Avon
Lavenham
Cambridge
Ledbury
Broadway
CROWN
Gloucester
Luton
Colchester
HOOPS INN
GEORGE
GEORGE
RED LION
Amersham
ANGEL
LUTTERELL ARMS
Lacock
Hurley
BELL
Reading
Bath
Norton St. Philip
Dunster
Guildford
ANGEL
NEW INN
Wylie
Clovelly
Horns Cross
Glastonbury
DELL QUAY
Chichester
STAR
Cullompton
Tarrant Monkton
Alfriston
Exeter
BELL INN
OLD FERRY INN
DOLPHIN
Bodinnick
LANGTON ARMS
MANOR HOUSE
Sennen
FIRST & LAST
Miles
0
20
40
60
80
100
N

I Old English Inns

THE old English inn is still one of our main romantic delights. It is a picturesque gateway into the past, taking us down long and fascinating perspectives of social history. It invites us, perhaps by some flavour or reminiscence of the Middle Ages, to identify ourselves with Chaucer's pilgrims, or to join the company of some Tudor noble travelling between his country house and the Court; to share the excitement of arrival and departure with a coach party and the Rowlandson characters of the Regency; to enter into the spirit of Dickensian adventure.

The associations of these old inns are indeed endless and they themselves exist in a rich variety and such numbers as to offer, even today, a field of exploration virtually without limit, though so many are famous alike for their architecture and tradition. In an ancient town the inn, standing at its very centre, is often next only in architectural dignity and interest to the church. Whether it has such an opulence of timbered "black-and-white" as that of the "Bear and Billet" at Chester or the Georgian spaciousness and restraint of the "Dolphin" at Chichester, it is an essential part of that town nucleus to which the traveller comes with all the relief of one who has got to the heart of things and found the basic symbols of a way of life.

Architecturally, too, the inn is often an exquisite example of the use of local building materials—nowadays so often advocated and too seldom practised—thus giving that appropriateness to its setting of which the "Lygon Arms" at Broadway is so fine an example. A thatched and half-timbered inn in the New Forest, a plain little inn of stone among mountains, can equally be pleasurable to view in belonging naturally to the landscape where they are found, and some that are scarcely more than cottages have all the local character that gives to old cottages a peculiar beauty. To this individuality of appearance we must add the individuality of names and signs, another aspect of the inn's fascination; in itself a wonderful compound of historical allusion, poetic inventiveness and curious craft, not to speak of verbal mysteries, agreeable to contemplate or solve.

It is not out of place to consider at this point what exactly constitutes an inn and why the word has so grateful and welcoming a sound to the ear. Strictly speaking, it is to be distinguished from the tavern or alehouse and an essential difference from them is contained in the word "inn" itself, closely related as it is to the preposition "in" and capable of use as a verb (transitive or intransitive) meaning "to lodge" or "put up", being so used by Chaucer. The inn was a place of sojourn for travellers, pilgrims and wayfarers. The tavern (as in a specific meaning of the Latin *taberna*) was a wine-shop; in Tudor times mainly to be found in the cities and larger towns for the retail of wine, though it might also provide cooked meals. The alehouse, in contrast, was an institution of the village or small community, though again it did not cater for travellers but simply dispensed ale to a local and rural custom.

Separate lines of development thus appear. The ancient tavern may be looked on as the forerunner of the eighteenth-century coffee-house, the prototype of the modern restaurant. The alehouse has changed little with the centuries. The development of the inn stretches impressively from the monastic hostelry to the modern hotel. It has always had a corresponding prestige and respect, for as one of the "wholesome observations" in a seventeenth-century broadside *Rules for Innkeepers* puts it "It must not be accounted a small matter to afford houseroom, lodging, rest and food to the comforts of God's children". The distinction in practice between the various kinds of "public house" (if the word is appropriate—for this too has its shade of separate meaning) has never been absolute. An eighteenth-century ruling by Richard Burn in his *Justice of the Peace* decides that "if an alehouse lodges and entertains travellers, it is also an inn". Before then, an Act of 1604 (quoted in a learned study of country inns and alehouses by Mr. R. H. Bretherton) seeks to group all together by a worthy purpose and separate them only by a deviation from it: "the ancient, true and proper use of Inns, Alehouses and Victualling Houses was for the Receipt, Relief and Lodging of Wayfaring People travelling from Place to Place . . . and not meant for the entertainment and harbouring of Lewd and Idle People to spend and consume their Money and Time in Lewd and Drunken Manner". It was certainly in the spirit of Christian benevolence and hospitality that the English inn had its origin, that is, in its connection with the religious houses of medieval times.

II Early Development

ONE could, of course, go farther back in history for a number of parallels. As a group of lodgings round a court or yard, there is some likeness to be traced between the caravanserais of the ancient East and such a specialized later form as our Inns of Court (which give their own venerable and dignified associations to the word "inn"). Some writers on the subject invite us to reflect on the places of lodging and entertainment with which the Romans must have provided the province of Britain along with other Latin amenities, the posting houses or "mansiones" of the Roman roads, the "bibulia" or taverns of the Romano-British cities, though the only feature that survived after the Roman occupation was the sign, the Bacchic wreath or garland of vine leaves. As a green bush—the "ale-stake" of Chaucer—looking, in the Luttrell Psalter, like a broom with a long stick, it may be regarded as the original inn sign. There is no trace of the Saxon inn, though the monasteries which existed before the Norman Conquest presumably had some separate accommodation for guests. There are records or legends of the foundation of some between the twelfth and fourteenth centuries, but as far as actual structure or remaining structural detail is concerned it is necessary to jump to the fifteenth century. Thus the "Star" at Alfriston in Sussex was originally founded in the thirteenth century though its fabric dates from the latter part of the fifteenth. If it is only in the last phase of medieval England, that is, the period just preceding the Tudors, that the oldest inns we know take shape, some general characteristics then remaining must already have had a long history. There were in effect only two places to which travellers on a long-distance journey could repair, the castle or the abbey, priory or monastery. The monastic institutions built special quarters as an annexe for guests, sometimes resolving into three separate buildings, one for the distinguished, another for the middle class of pilgrims and a third for the humbler wayfarers. Plain but adequate fare was provided and accommodation was free, to give it being a Christian duty, though the Church was compensated indirectly in more than one way, by the benefactions of the wealthy and by the donations and contributions of pilgrims at the shrines they visited. Pilgrimage either as an act of piety or special effort to secure saintly intercession in some personal difficulty, and perhaps also as the only form of travelling holiday the Middle Ages offered, was popular in pre-Reformation England and no less popular in the disturbed period of the Wars of the Roses than when (a century before) Chaucer's nine and twenty pilgrims set out from the "Tabard" at Southwark for the other terminus inn, the "Checquers of the Hope", in Mercery Lane at Canterbury. The shrine of St. Thomas at Canterbury; of Our Lady of Walsingham in Norfolk; the abbey of Glastonbury where Joseph of Arimathea was said to have planted a graft from the Sacred Thorn; these were famous resorts, requiring the provision of lodgings, and the fact that one of the most beautiful and, in appearance, most medieval of inns, what is now the "George and Pilgrims Hotel" at Glastonbury (originally named simply after St. George) was built by Abbot John de Selwood at about the time of the battle of Barnet, shows how little the storms of Edward IV's reign affected an established custom.

Indeed, the disturbances of the period seem to have been a stimulus to travel and therefore to the growth of inns. Beset in their country estates by the robber barons and their armies, a new type of gentry, of which the Paston family gives the best-known example, were travelling constantly to London and the Court to seek legal protection and powerful support: many thousands of miles must John Paston have covered and at many a hostelry put up in his constant journeys from Norfolk to the capital. At the same time political history perhaps inclines us to see too sharp a social break at the advent of Henry VII. Inns were developing steadily, though peace and the growth of trade certainly quickened the process. It is interesting to study this development in a single building like the "Red Lion" at Colchester where many sixteenth-century additions were made, without any appearance of abrupt transition, to the structure of *c.* 1470. Obviously, however, a new era follows the Dissolution of the Monasteries by Henry VIII in 1536. Automatically it brought to an end the monastic inn or converted it into a secular establishment run by a landlord for profit. The Elizabethan and the Jacobean periods are a classic age of the inn, bequeathing many a half-timbered masterpiece of domestic architecture, like the "Falcon" at Stratford and the "Feathers" at Ledbury, and adding its richness to an earlier structure as in the "George" at Norton St. Philip. Many earlier inns were completely rebuilt, among them, though, alas, it is now only an illustrious name, the "Tabard" of Southwark. In itself it gives an epitome of inn history. Built by the Abbot of Hyde in 1307 as a pilgrims' inn adjoining his monastery's town hostel, it was sold into private hands by Henry VIII after the Dissolution, being described as "the Tabard of the Monastery of Hyde and the Abbot's place with the stables and garden thereto belonging". At the beginning of the seventeenth century it was still as Chaucer knew it, but was reconstructed in Elizabeth's time, and what survived the Great Fire of 1666 and lasted until the demolition of 1874 was of Elizabethan date.

In some main features the Elizabethan inn did not depart from the earlier type, though it was generally larger and in many respects improved. In the immemorial fashion it was built round a galleried courtyard (in which plays were often produced) approached by the main entrance gate. In another yard behind were the stables for the guests' horses and for the large covered waggons (almost caravans) in which the Tudor family of high degree could travel from place to place in some stateliness. The half-timber construction, typical of the centuries when England was more forested than now, and found more especially in the regions where the oak flourished, was not in itself new. No doubt many monastic guest houses, from the eleventh century onwards, like the cottages and farmhouses to which they are often more closely related in style than to ecclesiastical buildings, had this framework of timber posts and struts filled in with other material. There is not, however, much to go upon architecturally before the fifteenth century, and there is an evident increase in the century that followed not only of size but of an intended and decorative elaboration which sets the timbered Elizabethan inn in a class of its own. The number of rooms gave an added picturesqueness of effect in the shape of many and varied window spaces, for instead of the communal dormitories to which the pilgrims had been assigned guests now had their own rooms, often distinguished not by a number in the modern hotel fashion, but by some agreeably poetical name like the "Reine Chamber" and the "Flower-de-Luce Chamber" of the Elizabethan "Tabard".

One may assume a similar elaboration in the culinary and other interior equipment. In his standard work on *The Old Inns of England*, Professor Sir Albert Richardson quotes the inventory of the Elizabethan "Tabard" and its astonishing list of "kettles, pots, pans and basins of brass and copper . . . pot hooks, tongs, mincing-mills, griddles, frying pans and steamers, made of Sussex iron . . . pewter pots graded from the pottle to the gill, glasses, stone utensils and trenchers". It is with an appropriate feeling for the past that old inns collect and display, even if they have not inherited, the museum pieces of the kitchen and with a similar feeling that one views them.

The growth of towns and trade, rather than the improvement of roads and communications, accounts for the splendours of the Elizabethan inn. If people travelled for pleasure it was in spite of the hardships of the road. Perhaps to some extent it was a patriotic fashion to follow the example of the Queen herself whose notorious love of journeying about her realm has attached the tradition or legend to so many inns that "here Queen Elizabeth slept". At the same time, now that pilgrimage had ceased to give its special privilege and sanction, the humbler traveller attracted some suspicion, the "wayfarer" tended to be labelled a mere vagrant. Some kind of supervision became necessary, though this largely applied to the increase, with the growth of towns, of the taverns and alehouses, which at once constituted rivals to the inn and a source of concern to the authorities; in encouraging drunkenness and also as possible hotbeds of mischief and conspiracy. By the end of the sixteenth century the more frivolous places of entertainment outnumbered the inns proper by something like twelve to one. Anciently, because of their useful function the latter required no licence and those existing before 1552 were exempted from the licensing regulations then applied. The authorities, however, took what steps they could to discourage the establishment of either new inns or alehouses. Drunkenness, with the larger import of heavy wines and the substitution of strong beer for the watery "ale" of the Middle Ages, was becoming a problem. Philip Stubbs in his *Anatomie of Abuses* written towards the end of the sixteenth century tells us that "Every cuntrey, citie, towne, village & other hath abundance of alehouses, taverns & Innes which are so fraughted with maultworms, night & day, that you would wûnder to see them."

The efforts of the seventeenth century to discourage "maltworms" and the places which harboured them scarcely applied to the larger inns which had acquired considerable prestige. The topographer William Harrison in his *Description of England* (1587) had spoken with approval of these "great and sumptuous" establishments. The traveller Fynes Moryson in 1617 declared "The Worlde affoords not such Innes as England hath, either for good and cheape entertainment after the Guests owne pleasure or for humble attendance upon passengers." Civil War and Puritan rule, however, must have given a pause to their extension in the middle years of the century. It was not until the Restoration that notable inns (such as the "Bell" at Stilton) were again built. On the other hand, official and puritanical efforts to check the growth of taverns and alehouses seem to have had the contrary effect of producing an obstinate and defiant increase. No effective check proved possible on the local growth of the borderline alehouse-inns, often converted dwelling-houses in then remote villages which might (but more probably would not) give accommodation to the traveller. That amusing oddity, the ex-Thames waterman John Taylor, the "Water Poet" describes at length in 1649 his failure to find a night's lodging in any of the six alehouses in "a fisher town called Megaveasie" where he was treated like "some strange Beast or Monster brought out of *Africa*". Their principal purpose was, as it has remained, that of a local exchange of news and views and relaxation after work. Without any remarkable external features the vast number still existing today include many that date from this century and their relative and unpretentious antiquity has its own distinct charm for the eye.

III The Georgian Phase

IT is the Georgian age, and more especially the late Georgian, that gives us the next great period of the inn. The definite architectural change then observable was, of course, due to the same factors as affected other buildings and architecture in general. The Great Fire had left its convincing argument against the old form of timber construction in towns, but the revulsion of taste against the quaint and anything that still savoured of medieval barbarism must also be reckoned with. This bore especially hard on the inn. Not only were new hostelries built of brick or stone but on the front of existing buildings these materials were used to cover over and hide from view what was considered the lamentable evidence of the ignorant past. Thus many delightful Tudor fronts were bricked and plastered over and their very existence forgotten, the humbler rear premises alone retaining the outward signs of antiquity. Often it is only in comparatively recent times that the original work has been revealed. Simplicity and good proportion took the place of the old rambling ornateness. In its more modest form the Georgian inn resembled a plain and unpretentious farmhouse, though on a larger scale, and as their prosperity grew in the later years of the eighteenth century, some acquired the aspect of a mansion, this effect being confirmed by the dignity of a columned porch; as well as being a sign of current architectural taste, a tactful suggestion that its patrons were of a superior order and that here was a fitting rendezvous for the meet of the local Hunt, or the assembly of local politicians for whom a special "Assembly Room" was often provided.

Yet as far as the main road inns were concerned, the old plan, being functional, was adhered to. The gateway leading to a courtyard was retained and in the first half of the century was still quite low, the day of the outside passenger not having yet arrived. The evolution of the coach in design and the popularity of outside seats led to the construction of larger and more impressive archways at the end of the eighteenth and the beginning of the nineteenth century, while a second way out at the rear of the inn enabled the coach to get swiftly off the mark and on the road again.

To understand the development of the inn at this period it is, indeed, necessary to consider the development of the road and its vehicles and in particular of the coach. In England the coach seems first to have appeared in Elizabethan times, and then slowly developed as a public conveyance, though it was not until the eighteenth century that it became an important form of transport, as distinct from the cumbrous four-wheeled vans and waggons that had been used to carry passengers and goods since the Middle Ages. The word "stage", of course, indicated the regular stopping-places on its route (i.e. inns) where horses were changed and passengers taken up and set down. Hogarth in his engraving of 1747 of a country inn yard at the "Old Angle" [*sic*] shows how primitive the stage-coach still was, a kind of enlarged sedan-chair on four heavy wheels with a boot for luggage comprising a passenger seat and a convex roof without protective rail or guard, on which the hardier or rougher type of traveller crouched as best he might: only the slow pace of the vehicle could have prevented him from losing his precarious hold.

The great change which so much affected the inn itself took place in the second half of the eighteenth century. The roads were improved, the introduction of turnpikes and tolls helping to finance local repair and construction. From then onwards, the design, number and speed of the stage-coaches advanced with road improvement—the latter reaching its height with the new constructions of Macadam and Telford in the early nineteenth century. The post was an important factor. It was long conveyed by relays of "post-boys" but the "mail-coach", taking over the function of the old post-boys, was introduced in 1784. Springs, the lack of which must have made earlier journeys an ordeal, came into use in 1789 and soon afterwards the whole type of construction was overhauled to produce a light coach built for speed as well as to provide the maximum convenience for passengers inside and out. The great coaching era may thus be dated from *c.* 1780 to *c.* 1840 (when the railways were ousting them) and this was also another great era of the inn. New ones were built, the old lavishly and drastically reconstructed all along the elaborate system of roads that now radiated over the country, north, south, east and west. The Regency period, and the reign of George IV, that is, from 1810 to 1830, mark a zenith of the inn's prosperity. The road travel on which it was based has several aspects. For one thing what may be called the "discovery of England" was in full swing. Poets and painters, antiquaries and archaeologists (professional and amateur) were scouring the land to seek out, describe and depict the castles, abbeys and churches and other remnants of the now romantically interesting past. Then, during the Napoleonic wars, there was an obvious need for swift communication between the capital and all parts of the country. Again, the first Industrial Revolution was taking effect. There was a movement of population from the countryside into the cities and towns, growing with unprecedented speed; while commerce and industry sent their agents to and fro in ever-increasing numbers. Speedy travel was a commercial and industrial need. During the late Georgian period it was also a sporting amusement, like a modern automobile race; the coach was patronized by enthusiastic Corinthians and the coaching prints of the time, it may be noted, are classified as a form of sporting print.

Thus an air of bustle, excitement and hospitable preparation pervaded the main road inns. The arrival and departure of the coach was the great event of day or night. Meals were served with a promptitude matching the punctuality of the coach's own time-table. The Regency dining-room into which the guests are ushered is lofty, with tall windows cheerfully draped with red plush curtains, made elegant by touches of classic detail, heightened with gold, while a sporting flavour is added by the pictures on the walls, aquatints of coaching scenes after James Pollard or William Shayer or of racing scenes after Henry Alken or John Sartorious. The ten outside, the eight inside, passengers sit down (with some nice social distinctions) to long tables, while a tempting array of hot food is ready for them, brought by scurrying waiters.

That delightful artist, Pollard—so masterly in his own field, so minor outside it as to be virtually unknown—has depicted with lively and authentic detail every phase of the epic of arrival and departure; the four horses daintily stepping into the yard as if to prove their freshness after a spirited run, waiter and ostler advancing to perform their respective duties; the caped and cloaked figures warming themselves by a roaring fire; in the breakfast room—as the others discuss game pie and mulled ale—the gentleman who with homely informality is being shaved in one corner.

How many eulogies have been written—like that of Mrs. Gore—of the "Inns of good dimension and repute, where the mail-coach supped or dined, and the great northern families stopped to sleep; where portly sirloins, huge rounds of beef, hams of inviting complexion, fowls, supportable even after those of dainty London, spitch-cocked eels and compotes of wine-sours were evermore forthcoming on demand. What home-brewed—what home-baked—what cream cheese—what snow-white linen—what airy chambers—and what a jolly-faced old gentleman, and comely old gentlewomen to bid you welcome. It was a pleasure to arrive—a pain to depart." That there was some social discrimination in this benignity, tending to direct it to the superior order of traveller and withhold it from others, cannot be denied. Thomas De Quincey, who so wonderfully evoked the dash and excitement of journeying by coach, notes, with his accustomed humour, the different treatment extended to the "illustrious quaternion" of four inside people and the three miserable "outsides"—"outsiders" in every sense of the word—who "made a vain attempt to sit down at the same breakfast table with the consecrated four", and were briskly dealt with by the waiter who "sang out 'This way, my good men' and then enticed these good men away to the kitchen".

Dusty and way-worn, Karl Phillip Moritz, German pastor and traveller in England in 1782, arrived at an inn and was promptly assessed as kitchenworthy only and set down to sup "at the same table with some soldiers and the servants". It was with a certain pique that while he was eating he became aware that a post-chaise had driven up and that instantly the whole house was set in motion "in order to receive with all due respect, these guests who were no doubt supposed to be persons of consequence". On the other hand he was "in one of those kitchens which I had so often read of in Fielding's fine novels", and his description well conveys its spaciousness and abundant interest. "All round on the sides were shelves with pewter dishes and plates and the ceiling was well stored with provisions of various kinds, such as sugar loaves, black puddings, hams, sausages, flitches of bacon, etc."

To the modern eye, indeed, the inn kitchen can be quite entrancing. The core of the establishment, it was very often architecturally the sole relic of some earlier building. If the vision of the socially misunderstood writer has sometimes been jaundiced, that of the painter and draughtsman has never failed to delight in the inn kitchen, the spits, the pots and pans, the wealth of still-life. Thomas Rowlandson is as cheerfully at home by the wide chimney, among the cooking utensils, the kitchenmaids and ostlers, as with the gay company that sits down to a hunt supper in an "assembly room" above. If one seeks a modern example of the artist's delight in the inn kitchen, there is Fred Elwell's circumstantially detailed painting of the "Beverley Arms" and that magnificent kitchen which antedates the otherwise eighteenth-century hotel.

IV The Inn in Literature

THE art and the literature associated with inns provide a large and interesting study. All English literature is seamed with references to them, appearing in the journals of travellers and social observers, in plays, poems and novels, in scattered eulogy and epigram. Rich cream of quotation is to be found in fulness in the admirable books of Thomas Burke and Sir Albert Richardson, yet it is not possible to omit even in a short essay some of the classic examples they have cited at length or to add others from an almost inexhaustible store. From the fourteenth century, the written word remains when the buildings have gone, and two men of contrasting genius evoke for us the atmosphere of the inn and, also, in contrast, of the alehouse or tavern. In a few words Chaucer conveys the size and amenity of the "Tabard" where

The chambres and the stables weren wyde
And wel we weren lodged at the beste.

Langland in Piers Plowman, however, describes no less effectively though more harshly, the ditchers, scavengers, cobblers and tinkers who pass the cup round in an alehouse interior that one feels Teniers might have painted.

Skelton, Shakespeare, Ben Jonson, Izaak Walton, Pepys, Defoe, Swift, Addison, Pope, Dr. Johnson, Goldsmith, Fielding, Smollett, De Quincey, Hazlitt, Washington Irving, Dickens, together with a host of lesser and more recent chroniclers, bring the inn in their various ways to vivid life. In a simplified anthology one might place first those general terms of praise which are so famous, and give first place to Dr. Johnson's remarks, which apply impartially to inn and tavern, after he had dined with Boswell "at an excellent inn at Chapel-House, where he expatiated on the felicity of England in its taverns and inns and triumphed over the French for not having in any perfection the tavern life. 'There is no private house (said he) in which people can enjoy themselves so well as at a capital tavern . . . there is a general freedom from anxiety. You are sure you are welcome and the more noise you make, the more trouble you give, the more good things you call for, the welcomer you are. No servants will attend you with the alacrity which waiters do who are incited by the prospect of an immediate reward in proportion as they please. No, Sir; there is nothing which has yet been contrived by men by which so much happiness is produced as by a good tavern or inn." He then repeated with great emotion, Shenstone's lines:

Whoe'er has travell'd life's dull round,
Where'er his stages may have been,
May sigh to think he still has found
The warmest welcome at an inn.

"We happened to lie this night", Boswell adds, "at the inn at Henley where Shenstone wrote these lines" (the "Red Lion").

Hazlitt in his essay *On Going a Journey* adds another laudatory gem . . . "How fine it is to enter some old walled town, walled and turreted just at the approach of nightfall, or to come to some straggling village, with the lights streaming through the surrounding gloom; and then after inquiring for the best entertainment that the place affords, to 'take one's ease at one's inn'. These eventful moments in our lives' history are too precious, too full of solid, heart-felt happiness to be frittered and dribbled away in imperfect sympathy . . ." Well known as they are, these magnificent assertions of Johnson, Shenstone and Hazlitt surround the inns we visit with their own atmosphere.

Then there is "mine host" as he appears in literature: the type is established by Henry Bailly of the *Canterbury Tales*, the lay landlord and organizer of pilgrimage, the "man of merry words" who chaffs the silent poet with his downcast eyes. The tradition of geniality is continued in the cheerful and somewhat fantastic host of the "Garter" in Shakespeare's *The Merry Wives of Windsor*. A host as careless, as merry, is described by John Taylor, the Water Poet, at the "Rose and Crown" at Nether Stowey, a man of "delightful and hydropical nonsense" who "swigged off half a pot to me and asked me if I would have any powdered beef and carrots for supper" (though it eventually turned out that he had none or indeed anything else eatable). The Will Boniface of Farquhar's *The Beaux' Stratagem* is the persuasive host who extols his ale as being "smooth as oil, sweet as milk, clear as amber, and strong as brandy and will be just fourteen years old on the fifth day of next March, old style". They are notable characters, whether in fact or fiction, though observers at different periods have found them of different kinds. At the "Sign of the Great Omega" an Elizabethan traveller, quoted by the Hon. John Byng, found an exemplary scene—"the goodman, his two sons, his chamberlain and his hostler singing the CIV Psalm of David very distinctly and orderly; the goodwife with her two daughters sat spinning at their wheels a little distance from them". He was received with equally exemplary courtesy. One might contrast with this, William Cobbett's account of his visit to the "George Inn" at Andover "kept by one Sutton, a rich old fellow who wore a round-skirted sleeved fustian waistcoat, with a dirty white apron tied round his middle and no coat on; having a look the *eagerest* and the *sharpest* that I ever saw in any set of features in my whole lifetime" who tried to stop Cobbett from a lengthy harangue in the dining-room because it interfered with his sale of liquor. It was the fate of Karl Moritz to meet with "haughty and insolent airs", though one landlord at Windsor received him "with great civility and even kindness"—not matched, however, by that of the waiters and maids who looked on the pedestrian foreigner as "a scandal and an eyesore".

Adventure, however, that is, the unexpected and unpredictable, was always part of the charm of the inn, and if the good ones were delightful the bad were often at least amusing. Pepys, whose diary is studded with the names of inns and taverns, enjoys the comfort of the "George" at Salisbury "where lay in a silk bed and very good diet" but seems also to have derived entertainment from the little inn where he found "the beds good but lousy, which made us merry". The "Water Poet" describes with considerable gusto the horrors of the inn at Nether Stowey, with its "Ethiopian army of fleas", its walls and ceilings "adorn'd and hanged with rare Spider's Tapstry, or Cobweb Lawne". Washington Irving writes with equal pleasure of the best and worst. He could admire to the full "that picture of convenience, neatness and broad honest enjoyment, the kitchen of an English inn . . .", the "hams, tongues and flitches of bacon suspended from the ceiling", the "smoke-jack [which] made its ceaseless clanking beside the fire-place", the "well-scoured deal table . . . with a cold round of beef, and other hearty viands upon it, over which two foaming tankards of ale seemed mounting guard". He could also derive exquisite sensation from the tedium of a wet Sunday in 1822 at an inn in "the small town of Derby". "The rain pattered against the casements, the bells tolled for church with a melancholy sound. . . ." The American visitor gazed out hopelessly on the sodden debris and puddles of the stable-yard. "It was quite refreshing when in the course of the morning a horn blew and a stage-coach whirled through the street, with outside passengers stuck all over it, cowering under cotton umbrellas and seethed together and reeking with the steam of wet box-coats and upper benjamins. The sound brought out from their lurking-places a crew of vagabond boys and vagabond dogs and the carroty-headed ostler and that nondescript animal yclept Boots and all the other vagabond race that infest the purlieus of an inn" though as the coach set off again the vagabond race disappeared and once more tedium reigned supreme.

It was an adventure for Moritz, reaching Oxford at midnight and hobbling with little appreciation along the "longest, finest and most beautiful street in Europe", to find himself unexpectedly admitted at the "Mitre" into the company of a party of clerical gentlemen, dons it might be assumed, "all with their gowns and bands on, sitting round a large table, each with his pot of beer before him" and indulging in scholiast argument concerning the Scriptures worthy of the learned fantasies of Mr. Michael Innes. As a setting for adventurous happenings the playwright and novelist have made constant use of the inn. We are bidden to laugh at the confusion of travellers, misdirected and treating the local mansion as an inn, as in Goldsmith's *She Stoops to Conquer*, or such another celebrated confusion as that at the "Great White Horse" at Ipswich where Mr. Pickwick had his embarrassing encounter with the lady in yellow curl-papers. For Tom Brown in *Tom Brown's Schooldays*, setting out to Rugby for the first time, the adventures of the road were a stirring prelude to those of school—and what a cosy glimpse its author, Thomas Hughes, gives of the "Peacock" at Islington where Tom's father orders supper of steaks and oyster sauce: and of the sporting inn farther on the way with "the low, dark wainscoted room hung with sporting prints . . . the quaint old glass over the mantelpiece in which is stuck a large card with the list of the meets for the week of the county hounds; the table covered with the whitest of cloths and of china and bearing a pigeon pie, ham, round of cold boiled beef cut from a mammoth ox, and the great loaf of household bread on a wooden trencher . . ."

Inn fare, indeed, though there are naturally exceptions, gets very good marks from the travellers of the past, and more particularly of the coaching age. Southey, it is true, writing in the disguise of a Spanish traveller in his *Letters from England* of 1807, remarks of the food provided "they eat their meat half raw; the vegetables are never boiled enough to be soft; and everything is insipid except the bread, which is salt, bitter and disagreeable". Yet the plenty of the inn in the coaching heyday made other observers quite lyrical—Disraeli pictures it ornately—"What a profusion of substantial delicacies! What mighty and iris-tinted rounds of beef! What vast and marble-veined ribs! What gelatinous veal pies! What colossal hams! Those are evidently prize cheeses! And how invigorating is the perfume of those various and variegated pickles! . . ." Though suffering many disappointments in the course of his travels between 1781 and 1794, the Hon. John Byng was mellowed at the "White Hart", Broadway (later called the "Lygon Arms") by its "delicious loin of veal", the "superabundant temptation" of its apricot tart.

Many are the memorable descriptions of exterior and interior. Shakespeare calls up for us the rooms with fancy names, the wall-paintings (in style, no doubt, resembling those uncovered at the "White Swan", Stratford-on-Avon). It was in "my Dolphin-chamber", says the hostess, in *Henry IV*, Part II, addressing Falstaff, "thou didst swear to me on a parcel-gilt Goblet . . . at the round table, by a sea-coal fire, on Wednesday in Whitsun week, when the Prince broke thy head for liking his father to a singing man of Windsor". Falstaff's own idea of decoration was "for thy walls a pretty, slight Drollery or the Story of the Prodigal, or the German hunting in Waterwork [i.e. distemper paint] is worth a thousand of these Bed-hangings and these fly-bitten Tapestries". It is in such a setting that we find him again at the "Garter" inn in *The Merry Wives of Windsor*, the Host directs Simple to Falstaff's "Chamber, his House, his Castle, his standing-bed and truckle-bed: 'tis painted about with the story of the Prodigal, fresh and new". In *Henry IV*, Part I, comes also that famous scene in an inn-yard at Rochester where the carriers stumble out with their lanterns before dawn ("Charles's wain is over the new chimney") groaning and complaining that this "is the most villainous house in all London Road for Fleas".

Of the neat and homely aspect of the small country inn there are charming literary pictures, like that of the "Thatched House" at Hoddesdon where *Piscator* in Izaak Walton's *The Compleat Angler* looks forward to a "cleanly room with lavender in the windows and twenty ballads stuck about the wall". Goldsmith in

The Deserted Village gives in words the equivalent of a George Morland painting in his description of the inn-parlour with

> *The white-washed wall, the nicely sanded floor*
> *The varnished clock that clicked behind the door . . .*
> *The pictures placed for ornament and use,*
> *The twelve good rules the royal game of goose . . .*
> *While broken tea-cups, wisely kept for show,*
> *Ranged o'er the chimney glistened in a row.*

One might compare with it Smollett's description of the "Black Lion" in *Sir Lancelot Greaves*, its kitchen "the only room for entertainment in the house, paved with red bricks, remarkably clean, furnished with three or four Windsor chairs, adorned with shining plates of pewter, and copper saucepans, nicely scoured . . . while a cheerful fire of sea-coal blazed in the chimney".

For exciting contrast there is the magnificence of the Adam ballroom, existing in actuality, of the "Lion", Shrewsbury, in which De Quincey slept (bedrooms being in course of redecoration) prior to his youthful flight to London. He speaks of its "noble proportions, lighted, if I chose to issue some orders, by three gorgeous chandeliers, not basely wrapped up in paper but sparkling through all their crystal branches, and flashing back the soft rays of my tall, waxen lights . . ." its spaciousness becoming tremendous in his romantic imagination as he lay in the dark, thinking of the arrival of the coach and adventure to come.

Dickens, too, stayed at the "Lion" in the old-fashioned annexe to the stately main building, where he noted "the windows bulge out over the street as if they were little stern windows of a ship. And a door opens out of the sitting-room on to a little open gallery with plants on it, where one leans over a queer old rail." The comments of Dickens on inns are as many as famous. Something of a sentiment for them he derived from the eighteenth-century novelists who were his early reading, more perhaps from the experience of his young days as a reporter, from 1831 to 1835, when "there never was anyone connected with newspapers who, in the same space of time, had so much express and post-chaise experience as I". He combined the observant habit of the reporter with the romantic feeling for the old and fantastic with the gorgeous results to be found throughout the novels. The picturesque reaches its height in the oft-quoted account of the "Maypole" in *Barnaby Rudge*, inspired by the Elizabethan inn the "King's Head", Chigwell, with its "more gable ends than a lazy man would care to count on a sunny day; huge zigzag chimneys out of which it seemed that even smoke could not but choose to come in more than naturally fantastic shapes imparted to it in its tortuous progress". Even his unfavourable comments on existing inns, stamped with his genius, have become favourable advertisement, the delight of both establishment and guests. No one else perhaps could liken the horse above the porch of the "Great White Horse" at Ipswich to "an insane cart-horse" yet it is this exuberant fancy that makes all Dickens inns, in G. K. Chesterton's approving adjective, "uproarious". The "labyrinths of uncarpeted passages, such clusters of mouldy, ill-lighted rooms, such huge numbers of small dens for eating in and sleeping in" as he found at Ipswich, are romantically fascinating. Impossible here to enumerate all the inns drawn "from life" or freely adapted from existing places in the novels of Dickens, one can only suggest the extent of this pleasant research by reference to the *Pickwick Papers* alone and briefly refer to the "Bull" at Rochester, which gained Mr. Jingle's terse encomium "—good house—nice beds—Wright's next house, dear—very dear—half a crown in the bill if you look at the waiter—", the "Leather Bottell" at Cobham where Mr. Tupman tippled, the "Great White Horse" at Ipswich already mentioned, the inns on Mr. Pickwick's journey in company with Benjamin Allen and Bob Sawyer, the "Bush", Bristol, the "Bell", Berkeley Heath, the "Hop-Pole", Tewkesbury, where they dined, the "Saracen's Head" (possibly the "Rose and Crown" at Sudbury) where the rival Eatanswill editors fought their battle, the "Angel" at Bury St. Edmunds where Mr. Jingle and his servant planned Mr. Pickwick's discomfiture—not to speak of the vanished "Golden Cross" at Charing Cross where the story begins or the "George and Vulture" in Castle Street where Mr. Pickwick stayed.

In addition to the inns described by writers there are those in which they wrote or where they visited or stayed. Shakespeare and Ben Jonson make imperishable the memory of the London "Mermaid", the latter speaks not only of great nights there but of the coteries and pretended wits—"your Three Cranes, Mitre and Mermaid men". In imagination we follow Shakespeare to the "Falcon" at Bidford-on-Avon and may speculate whether he wrote some part of *A Midsummer Night's Dream* at what was once the "Ship" in Grendon Underwood, Buckinghamshire. We know for certain that Dr. Johnson stayed at the "Three Crowns" in Lichfield, next his birthplace, as well as at the "Chapel House" where he made his famous pronouncement on tavern felicity. We follow Pepys to many an inn, the "George", Salisbury, as previously mentioned, the "Horseshoe", Bristol—"there trimmed by a very handsome fellow, 2s.", the "Three Tuns", Cambridge, "where we drank pretty hard and many healths to the King" and so on. In the ballroom of the old "Angel" at Basingstoke, Jane Austen danced and at the "Jolly Farmer" in Farnham, where he was born, William Cobbett no doubt first conceived the plan of his *Rural Rides*. Washington Irving is especially associated with the "Red Horse" at Stratford-on-Avon, Wordsworth and Scott have their link with the "Swan", Grasmere. Dickens wrote some part of *Dombey and Son* while staying at the "Albion", Broadstairs. Both Cardinal Newman and Charles Kingsley stayed at the "White Hart", Whitchurch, in Hampshire. It was by the "Barley Mow" at Wittenden, on the Thames, that Jerome K. Jerome moored the punt of *Three Men in a Boat*—in that book referring to its "story-book appearance" and its "once-upon-a-timeyfied interior"—while in more recent times as a literary innkeeper Mr. John Fothergill has given a particular celebrity to the "Spread Eagle" at Thame.

V Signs and Names

THE names and signs of inns, on which whole books have been written, might be looked on as a special form of the literature and art associated with them, so full are they of history, humour, poetry and symbolism. The "Bush", derived from the Roman circlet of ivy and vine leaves, is evidently the parent sign, the "ale-stake" of the Middle Ages, a standardized advertisement like the barber's pole. A grille or trellis over the window painted red was another early general mark of identification and as late as Elizabethan times, according to Dekker, "a whole street is in some places but a continuous ale-house not a shop to be seen between red lattice and red lattice". Yet the inn early developed individual dignity, the medieval connection with religious houses suggested an appropriate device, the "Cross", the "Cross Keys" (of St. Peter), the "Star" (of Bethlehem), the "Angel", the "Mitre", the symbol of St. Catherine—the "Catherine Wheel" which the Puritans are surmised to have corrupted into the "Cat and Wheel". The combination of piety and patriotism made the patron saint of England an obvious choice, accounting for the "George", the "George and Dragon" and perhaps the "Dragon" *solus*, though the derivation, as regards the latter, may have been from the Welsh Dragon of the Tudors or its other heraldic use. Some have speculated on a pagan survival in the sign of the "Sun" but this perhaps is as distant and indirect as the appearance of the sun symbol on old horse brasses, though these too may have had some influence on the character of inn signs.

The individuality of name was not merely a matter of taste and fancy. As early as the reign of Richard II signs were compulsory, and an indication of privilege as well as a requirement, for pulling down the sign was official notice of suppression; "For which gross Fault" we find in Massinger's *A New Way to pay Old Debts* ". . . I wil in mine own person, Command the constables to pull down thy sign". Where, as in a town, there might be several inns not far apart, there was an obvious advantage in a mark that at once proclaimed separate identity and, as in the lists or at court, heraldry served this purpose. The coat of arms, crest or badge of the reigning house or of the nobility provided loyal emblems. Thus the "White Hart" derives from the badge of Richard II, the "Swan" from the House of Lancaster, the "Falcon" from that of York. The "Greyhound" is a Tudor symbol, the "Talbot" refers to that breed of dog, appearing in the arms of the Earls of Shrewsbury. The "Bear and Ragged Staff" of the Earls of Warwick gives us many a "Bear" and, no doubt, Chester's "Bear and Billet". The *lion gules* of John of Gaunt gives us the "Red Lion" in profusion.

The inn name and sign has always paid its respect to royalty as the "Crown", the "Sceptre", the "King's Arms", the "Queen's Arms" indicate. The "Feathers" and "Plume of Feathers" are those of the Prince of Wales while from time to time foreign royalty has received acknowledgement, the "Dolphin" for instance referring to the arms of the French Dauphin, while admiration for Frederick the Great accounts for the "King of Prussia". The inn would also declare its attachment to the local great family, adopting its arms as a gesture of esteem and to indicate also its own status as an essential part of the local constitution. Thus we have the "Luttrell Arms" and the "Lygon", and even a small village inn like that at Tarrant Monkton proudly bears its heraldic device.

Yet the sources and variety of names are immensely varied, England is full of old "New Inns" which at one time or another replaced some earlier structure. Historic events and personalities have added their quota of titles—the "Royal Oak" refers to the escape of Charles II, the "Marquis of Granby" commemorates the distinguished soldier of the eighteenth century, now remembered rather by inn signs than by his presence at the battle of Minden. After the Napoleonic wars, the Duke of Wellington and Lord Nelson were obvious choices for the patriotic innkeeper. Food and drink have provided their tempting suggestion as in the "Cheshire Cheese" or the "Yorkshire Stingo", while the "Hoops" no doubt suggests, generally, the beer barrel or perhaps more particularly the bands at equal intervals on a quart pot. The association with the road obviously gives the "Coach and Horses" and sport the "Fox and Hounds", the "Fisherman's Rest" and the "Sportsman's Inn"; country occupations, the "Plough", the "Shepherd and Flock", the local site such descriptive names as the "Old Ferry Inn" or the "Pleasure Boat" of Hickling Broad. The "First and Last" at Sennen, a mile from Land's End, is, or was, the last to come to from the land, the first from the sea.

There remain besides many names of a grotesque, humorous and sometimes puzzling character, inciting ingenious explanation, the "Pig and Whistle" being a classic example, which has been thought a corruption of "Piggin o'Wassail" (or bowl of spiced ale) or of "Pyx and Housel" (Housel being the consecrated wafer of the Mass) but may as well be as simple a fancy as the cat and the fiddle of nursery rhyme. Probably many such fanciful combinations had no more meaning and purpose than to arouse the curiosity of passers-by or to leave with the visitor some distinctive and slightly jocular memory of the house in question.

As works of craftsmanship, signs were already elaborate in the sixteenth century. Harrison in 1587 remarks on their gorgeousness "wherein some do consume thirtie or fortie pounds, a mere vanitie in my opinion" though of this early splendour there is now little trace. The wooden effigy of angel or saint, once placed on the projecting corbel of the "George" at Glastonbury, like the figurehead of a ship, has long disappeared. The famous sign of the "White Hart" at Scole, fantastic arch across the roadway, richly carved in the seventeenth century with representations of Diana and Actaeon, was torn down during the Victorian period. The little stone carving of a convivial scene at the "Greenhouse Inn" in Monmouthshire (1719) is perhaps the oldest sign extant. Signs have taken various forms; a beam across the road, like that of the "Fox and Hounds" at Barley, Hertfordshire, with its metal silhouettes of the hunt; the bracket sign, wrought iron and painted panel; the sign hanging on an upright post, again painted or fashioned in metal. There are still pleasant bits of old local ironwork to be found, though weather has always been hard on the painted sign and there can hardly be anything now to show the nature of the "most magnificent Collection" of signs, organized by way of a satire on art exhibitions by Bonnell Thornton in 1762, except for such frequent representations of eighteenth-century signs as we find in the paintings and engravings of Hogarth, like those of the "Adam and Eve" and the "King's Head" in his famous "March to Finchley", and the amusing panel attributed to him of the "Man with a Load of Mischief", the load being the drunken wife with her glass of gin.

The sign was perhaps work for the heraldic craftsman, the coach-painter, the "primitive" (one wishes there are more) rather than the painter of realistic pictures, though a number of well-known artists in the latter sense have tried their hand. It is doubtful, however, if any trace exists of the signs Crome is said to have painted in Norfolk, or of Morland's or Julius Caesar Ibbetson's. David Cox's sign for the "Royal Oak" at Bettws-y-Coed was preserved inside the inn. The graceful White Hart for the inn of that name at Witley by Birket Foster and Alfred Cooper has its permanence in the Victoria and Albert Museum. Externally and in actual use, however, most signs are modern and are to be sampled as specimens of that revival the brewers and others have sought to bring about in recent years by using good painters. If a certain artistic politeness, not always in keeping with the hearty old English character of the inn, is sometimes to be found in them, there are many more examples in which good lettering, heraldic brightness of colour and some touch of whimsicality in design attain a satisfactory result.

VI Period of Decline

NO less dramatic than the expansion of inns in the coaching days is their decay with the coming of railways, or rather with their triumphant extension throughout the land. The first local lines made little difference to them; the Stockton and Darlington line of 1825, the Liverpool–Manchester, Newcastle–Carlisle and Whitstable–Canterbury lines, which followed in the space of a few years, made as yet no large threat to their existence; but from the 1840s onwards the amalgamation of lines, the new artificial roads of rail, signed the death-warrant of coach transport and in consequence condemned the coaching inns of the highroad to a prolonged period of decline and neglect. For a while the wealthy and conservative still "posted" from place to place in their own carriages, yet the convenience of railway travel was not to be denied by the staunchest lover of old ways. The sporting artist J. F. Herring in 1844 paints the York to Lincoln coach in the yard of the "Stamford Inn", but already as a gesture to the past, the figures wearing the costume of an earlier day. As the age of steam developed, traffic dwindled on all the stage-coach's once glamorous routes—the Dover, Portsmouth and Brighton Roads, the Oxford Road, the Bath Road, the Norwich and Ipswich Roads, the Holyhead Road, the Great North and North-West Roads—blight fell on the inns along them. Gone was the daily expectancy and excitement, the parade of ostlers, the bustle of waiters, the relays of tempting food. Crabbe gives a poetic picture of gloom and decay which would serve as a description of the havoc the railways had wrought

> *While you through large and dirty rooms proceed,*
> *Spacious and cold; a proof they once had been*
> *In honour—now magnificently mean;*
> *Till in some small half-furnished room you rest,*
> *Whose dying fires denote it had a guest.*

A different type of hostelry grew up, the Railway Hotel, as conveniently near a stopping place as the inns had formerly been on the highroad and with it the Commercial Hotel which had its advantage for the transient commercial traveller. In due course, perhaps, the *laudator temporis acti* will study the railway hotels, their palmy days and peculiar splendours with the affection now given to the inns they replaced or caused to decline, though the moment for this has scarcely yet arrived. What one notes, however, is the special fondness that the passing of an institution arouses, which created if not a new army of inn-users at all events a devoted band of inn-lovers as the nineteenth century approached its end, some of them cyclists like Charles G. Harper, one of our leading authorities, who pedalled all over England in the compilation of what he called his *Picturesque Account of the Ancient and Storied Hostelries of Our Own Country*.

With sighs of regret but also some of the satisfaction of a truly romantic research, Harper recorded how many inns, by the beginning of this century, had retired from business, been converted into farmhouses or houses stately enough to be called mansions, though retaining "some undefinable air" of their earlier character. There was "the immense, four-square, red-brick farmhouse" midway between Lichfield and Burton-on-Trent, once a coaching-and-posting-house famous in all that countryside as the "Flitch of Bacon"... the exclusive "Verulam Arms" at St. Albans, built in 1827 but ruined by the railways as early as 1837, a church being built on the space once occupied by its vast stables. On the Holyhead Road the casualties were especially numerous, the village of Brickhill was almost a ghost town of taverns. On the Great North Road, there was the "Haycock" at Wansford "in England" (famous since the seventeenth century for the often-told legend of "Drunken Barnaby", who was carried downstream on a haycock, and replied when asked where he came from, "Wansford in England", apparently under the impression he had reached some foreign clime). This was turned into a nobleman's shooting-box. The "Blue Bell" at Barnby Moor became a country seat, the "Swan" and "Angel" at Ferrybridge, "once great and prosperous coaching-houses" gave up and became ruinous. With the disappearance of coaches from the Brighton Road, the "Talbot" at Cuckfield long stood empty, the sign over its door: "You're welcome, what's your will?" becoming sadly ironic. On the Exeter Road, the "Raven", a seventeenth-century inn at Hook, became a private house in 1903. Then there was the great "Castle" inn at Marlborough, put out of business by the opening of the Great Western railway to Bath and Bristol in 1841, though finding a new lease of life as premises of Marlborough College in 1843. The "Chapel House" on the road to Worcester and Lichfield, where Dr. Johnson stayed, another great coaching inn, abandoned the struggle in 1850.

While making any such chronicle of dereliction, it is necessary, however, to remember that the old-established inns of the towns were for the most part able to survive, even though they suffered from the competition of the new hotels and the disappearance of the old road traffic. The smaller inns also, being supported by local trade rather than by the long-distance traveller, had a better chance of survival. An interesting instance of this is given by London itself (which may be viewed in one aspect as a collection of villages) where though the large historic inns have gone, there even now remain the smaller hostelries with a local character and a pre-Victorian picturesqueness, like the balconied inns of the river—the "Grapes", Limehouse, origin of Dickens's "Six Jolly Fellowship Porters" and that showpiece of today, the "Prospect of Whitby".

One must digress for a moment from fairly recent history to consider the quite separate tradition and character of the small and local establishment. There were the fishing inns, with their stuffed trout and pike in glass cases and their faithful circle of anglers; those with literary associations, like the "Swan" at Grasmere; those inns of the coast, once the haunt of smugglers, which have appealed to the imagination on this ground, like the old "Mermaid" at Rye; the lonely houses once the resort of or kept by highwaymen, like the "Golden Farmer" at Bagshot; as well as those which merely sustained the placid and unvarying current of social life in rural districts. The smugglers and the highwaymen were the phenomena of a period, so too the literary associations, yet the small inn became embalmed in their legend and if no legend existed was able to resist change to the same extent as the district in which it was found.

There is a curious contrast between the somnolent peace—not entirely happy seeing that it marked the depression of rural England in general—of the inn at the beginning of this century and the hectic glitter of the Victorian "public house" in the cities and towns now vastly enlarged by industry and commerce. All the features of the public houses were "modern". The division of public bar and "saloon", with other niceties of compartment, reflected new social distinctions. The cut glass, the imposing mahogany structures of the interior, gave an illusion of grandeur different from the homeliness of the inn proper. The essential difference remained that the "pub" was a place to drink in and not for the "receipt, relief and lodging" of travellers going from place to place. The revival of the inn was once more bound up with the number of these travellers and the revival of the road.

Cycling must be allowed its part in their rediscovery. One might almost speak of a "cycling age" of the road as an interim period in the old inn's reawakening. It seemed then to the explorers on two wheels as if the long period of neglect had induced a chastened kindliness of welcome into the host or hostess. The cyclist's tea with eggs and real cream for a shilling or less was their fare rather than the joints of beef that had awaited the coach passengers of old: their memories were of tiny, cleanly rooms under eaves of thatch, of the privilege they enjoyed as the advance-guard of revival sharing the road as yet only with the hay waggons and farm carts.

C. G. Harper speaks of those highways otherwise deserted, with their inns at which no other species of traveller seemed ever to pause. The petrol engine and the motor car, however, marked the decisive change in the fortunes of the inn, more especially from 1918 onwards. In a sense the present day, with its multitude of private cars and motor coaches, has revived in another guise the spirited panorama of the stage-coach and post-chaise days.

The effect on the old inn was not solely economic. Pride and interest in the structure of old buildings and the successive layers of their history was rekindled not only in visitors but in those who owned and managed them. There were discoveries to be made, great open fireplaces long concealed, old beams to be brought to light from beneath their covering of plaster and paper, external features similarly to be stripped of a featureless overlay. That a great deal of historic interest and beauty has been preserved by the Trust House organization in particular there is no doubt, and no account of old English inns in their present state can omit mention of the extraordinary growth of this undertaking from 1904 to the present day. As it has a commercial aspect it may be necessary to say that any remarks here made are entirely disinterested and concerned with the public value of what has been done. The idea of the Trust House was a return to the old tradition of providing food and lodging as distinct from merely providing liquor for sale, which during the long depression of the inn had become its main recourse. This project of the founder, the fourth Earl Grey, gained its great success on its own merits and of course also through the revival of road travel which in itself called for it. Yet from another point of view, the aims of the Trust House may be compared with those of the National Trust, though, of course, the two organizations are entirely distinct and independent of each other, and also with the aims of the Society for the Preservation of Ancient Buildings and the Society for the Preservation of Rural England, in the sense of maintaining to the best advantage buildings that were in their way historical monuments with a special architectural interest of their own. The more than 230 Trust Houses of today include many of the oldest and most interesting foundations in the country. Dating them either by record of origin or by the existence of some ancient structural features, one finds that at least one, the "Angel", Guildford, goes back to the thirteenth century, one, the "Blue Boar", Maldon, to the fourteenth century, eighteen to the fifteenth century, twenty-nine to the sixteenth century, twenty-two to the seventeenth century and thirty-five to the eighteenth century. They include such remarkable and famous buildings as the "Star", Alfriston, the "Red Lion", Colchester, the "Swan", Lavenham, the "Crown", Amersham, the "Luttrell Arms", Dunster, the "Dolphin", Chichester.

VII Approaches to the Inn

It would be tiresome to prescribe any systematic way of tracking down all the old inns of England, though a pleasant selection might be made on each of the main roads and old coaching routes. On the Great North Road one might pause to admire the Georgian "White Horse" at Eaton Socon in Bedfordshire, with its charming bow front, the (now by-passed) "Haycock" at Wansford in Northamptonshire, distinguished not only by the legend attached to its name but as one of the largest and most beautiful of seventeenth-century inns, the "Old Bell" at Stilton in Huntingdonshire, another stone-built seventeenth-century inn and one of the busiest in the coaching days, which first made Stilton cheese famous, and at Grantham the superb late medieval "Angel", where Richard III signed Buckingham's death-warrant, at Grantham noting also that most curious of inn-signs, the actual hive placed outside the "Beehive", also known as the "Living Sign". Then one might follow the course of the Roman Watling Street from London to the north-west along the Holyhead Road, pausing at Towcester to see the "Pomfret Arms", referred to in *Pickwick* as the "Saracen's Head" and the "Talbot", where Dean Swift stayed when Ireland-bound and where his chair is preserved, the "Lion" at Shrewsbury with its memories of Dickens and De Quincey. There is the Portsmouth Road to explore, already with its promise of the sea when still distant from the coast, in the "Anchors" of Ripley and Liphook. There is the Dover Road (the route of Chaucer's pilgrims) with the "Bull" at Rochester made famous by Dickens and the "Falstaffs" at Gadshill and Canterbury. At Dover itself one now finds the modern equivalent of the coaching inn, though startlingly transformed in its ultra-modern structure, the "Dover Stage", specially designed for present-day motor-coach traffic with the Continent.

Alternatively, one might take them county by county. They are fewer in number in the north and the industrial regions that were a nineteenth-century growth, yet Yorkshire offers some fine coaching inns like the "Golden Fleece" at Thirsk, the "Golden Lion" at Northallerton and the "Black Swan" at Helmsley. In Northumberland the "Lord Crewe Arms" at Blanchland is part of an extraordinary group of ancient buildings in a secluded cleugh of the northern moors that may be called unique. There is indeed no county without them; one might range from the "Tan Hill Inn" on the Yorkshire Pennines, 1,732 feet up, and at that height no doubt the loftiest in England, to the "Star" at Alfriston in its snug southern valley, a few miles from the Sussex coast, though the circle of counties round and nearer to London has perhaps the thickest clusters. Yet about any system of touring one might in the long run conclude that it is not really essential; the traveller in England comes inevitably on its old inns and there is indeed a special pleasure in the unpremeditated discovery of them in either the town or country district to which the visitor may have come for some quite other reason.

A non-geographical analysis suggests such questions as which are the oldest or the most beautiful and while these are almost unanswerable they provide an interesting inquiry. As to the "oldest", one has to distinguish between those that are actually old in structure and those, not necessarily so, which are old foundations, again discriminating in this latter case between the age testified by documentary record or known fact and that assumed from legend and tradition. A mellow and romantic feeling for "ye olde" rather than the cautious and scientific habit of the historian, accounts for such an inscription as Mr. George Long, F.R.G.S., found over the doorway of the "King and Tinker" in a winding country lane about two miles from Enfield

Established a thousand years.

It is possible that in origin the "Old Bell" at Finedon in Northamptonshire goes back to Saxon times as local tradition asserts, but it is an unquestionable fact that the building which survived into the twentieth century, with its statue of the Saxon Queen Editha, was Victorian Gothic of the completest kind. The delightful little "Fighting Cocks" at St. Albans, which the notice it bears describes as "The oldest inhabited house in the kingdom", also errs on the side of enthusiasm, for it is no more than part of a gateway to St. Alban's Abbey, half demolished when the Abbey was destroyed, a new roof and upper storey being added some time after the Dissolution in the sixteenth century. This would imply that the "Fighting Cocks" must rest content with the comparative youth of four hundred years. The "Trip to Jerusalem" at Nottingham is dated and described "1189 A.D. The oldest inn in England" but it is only the medieval suggestion of the title (which implies rather a halt on the way than a "trip" in the modern sense) that refers it back to the period of Richard I's crusades. There are also "Saracen's Heads" and "Turk's Heads" in plenty and they no doubt derived their names from crusading memory, yet Addison indicates how easily and without medieval connection they might appear at any time, when he describes how Sir Roger de Coverley, not wishing that a portrait of himself should be the sign of the village inn, caused moustachios to be painted on and the inn restyled the "Turk's Head". Several inns can with good reason claim a date of origin in the thirteenth or fourteenth century, but in the existing physical testimony of age perhaps the "George" at Norton St. Philip has the advantage, closely followed by such fifteenth-century glories as the "Angel", Grantham, the "George and Pilgrims", Glastonbury, and the "Red Lion", Colchester. Local patriotism and belief, however, must claim their indulgence and one would not wish to view coldly and sceptically Hilaire Belloc's assertion that the "Spread Eagle" at Midhurst in Sussex is "the oldest and most revered of all the prime inns of the world"—a superlative of true affection.

The sense of age or rather of continuity between past and present is more moving than the mere statement of date; the passage of three or four centuries made visible in the patchwork of an old inn is immensity of time enough.

To say which is the most beautiful of inns is another complex question, perhaps best answered by saying that most old inns are beautiful in their own fashion. There is certainly a special beauty, to which age contributes, in the half-timbered Tudor structure, for the warpings and variations of spacing thus produced in the old struts and beams have something of the ever-pleasing irregularity of nature itself, while some in their elaboration seem to represent a symbol of forest luxuriance, like the "Feathers" at Ledbury and the "Feathers" at Ludlow. There is another kind of appeal to the eye in the form of late Gothic represented by the "George and Pilgrims" at Glastonbury and the façade of the "Angel", Grantham, the latter in particular adapting the ecclesiastical style with great authority of design. In another category again are those inns notable for their stateliness and dignity of proportion, and in this respect the "Lygon Arms" at Broadway and the "Luttrell Arms" at Dunster are outstanding. The use of a local stone creates its own simplicity and harmony with its surroundings, though brick too has been used to stately effect as in the handsome gabled front of the "White Hart", Scole, Norfolk, built by a Norwich merchant in the seventeenth century.

Nor are the modest beauties of the small inn to be despised, so far from it indeed that the little thatched houses and the farmhouse and cottage-like structures without great pretension are often quiet works of art which claim a particular regard in themselves and, as may be seen in several of our illustrations, from their happy relation with their landscape setting. The old inns indeed, give their own commentary on the development and attractions of English domestic architecture. They cannot be completely distinguished from private houses and often enough have been originally designed as such, while some have reverted to that function. To explain that "undefinable air" which sets them somewhat apart from the purely domestic building one might refer in certain historic examples to their size or to the special purpose indicated by their archways and courtyards—apart from the signs and lettering which make their specific announcement—but perhaps most of all to those additions and combinations which reveal a growth like that of some natural organism. As an example, one might consider the front of the "Red Lion" at Colchester where Tudor panelling and a late Georgian bay window assort together with so little incongruity. It is only where some self-conscious and artificial imitation of an earlier style is imposed that incongruity appears, though until the nineteenth century respect for the past did not take this uncomfortable form. It is better that the new "Dover Stage" should be a structure characteristic of the present time in materials and aspect rather than some overgrown "olde" effort with fake half-timbering. On the other hand, this should not set up a contrary prejudice in appreciation against the genuine realities of Tudor construction, and the fact that what we are sometimes tempted to call "quaint" expressed purpose very well in terms of the methods and materials then in use.

That something of the beauty of old inns resolves into "atmosphere" is also true, a feeling of kinship and intimacy with the past, either stimulating or comforting, hardly separable from aesthetic appreciation. An old English inn is not merely a place to stay in temporarily but is in some way or other both a visual and emotional experience.

The "George and Pilgrims", Glastonbury

The inn now called the "George and Pilgrims", formerly the "George" simply, is a famous and precious relic of Gothic design as applied to a building of domestic use in the late medieval period. It was built, in the centre of the town, near Glastonbury Abbey by its Abbot, John de Selwood, *c.* 1470–5, mainly to accommodate the pilgrims who flocked to "the holyest earthe in England" where Joseph of Arimathea was said to have planted a graft from the Sacred Thorn. Its original title referred of course to St. George, whose cross appears on one of the three shields above the entrance, the second bearing the arms of Edward IV, the third (for the patron) being left blank, it would seem, because Abbot Selwood was without armorial bearings. The pilgrims who stayed at what he termed his "novum hospitium" were entertained free for two days and nights after which they were charged for their stay. The freestone front, so well planned that it looks much more spacious in area than its actual width of 34 feet, has survived to the present day almost without change. The pier and bracket which once bore a sculptured St. George and Dragon sign have undergone some alteration, the carved figure holding a cup (a medieval jest) is no longer in evidence in the battlement above the bay window but the panelled stonework has all its original perfection. The stone hall and staircase, the names given to rooms (the Abbot's Parlour, Abbot de Bere's Room, the Abbot's Kitchen), retain interior atmosphere, but the inner fittings of the inn in Selwood's time can now only be imagined. A finely dramatic legend relates that from one of the bedrooms Henry VIII, when the Dissolution of the Monasteries was in progress, watched the Abbey burn. The one substantial vestige of the Abbey's foretime splendour, its hostel, remains as clear-cut and cheering to the eye as some medieval illumination.

Photo: British Travel and Holidays Association

The "Star", Alfriston

The "Star" at Alfriston in Sussex ("best of primitive villages" in E. V. Lucas's words) is certainly one of the oldest and most interesting inns in England. If documents are lacking, there is every probability that it was once under the auspices of the Abbey of Battle, which is known to have owned property in Alfriston, and that one of its purposes was to house pilgrims bound for the shrine of St. Richard at Chichester, the Star (of Bethlehem) being the typical emblem of such monastic inns of the Middle Ages. The character of the front is authentically that of the fifteenth century (perhaps *c.* 1450), it was standing in this ancient village of the Cuckmere valley before America was discovered, or even before the Wars of the Roses had begun. Its delightful oriel windows, heavy timbering, the great slabs of Horsham stone which form the roof, and its unique carvings are all remarkable features.

The carvings, beneath the oriel windows, on the supporting bressummer beam and the ground floor front were no doubt the work of some minor ecclesiastical craftsman, the St. Michael (?) and Basilisk beneath the western window and the Shrine and Serpents of the central oriel suggesting a medieval church's misericord seats, while the grotesque heads on the bressummer beam, the lion and monkey on a corner post, the terrier dog, the mitred figure of an abbot or bishop, perhaps representing St. Giles with a wounded hart at his feet, are all in the same Gothic vein. More definitely, the fifteenth-century carving of the sacred monogram, IHS, on the upright wall-post supporting the main beam of the ceiling in the present bar parlour, proclaims religious intention. The oak entrance door of Tudor date, the Tudor hearth place of the bar parlour with its utensils of Sussex iron, and of the lounge where also an old roasting-jack is preserved add to the fascinating effect of this truly venerable building. A different order of carved grotesque, the lion that forms a corner post (figurehead from a Dutch ship wrecked off Birling Gap), does not, however in style and material, look out of character.

Photo: Trust Houses Ltd. (*A. C. K. Ware*)

TRUST
HOUSE
THE HISTORIC
STAR INN
LUNCHEONS
TEAS

The "George", Norton St. Philip

The "George" at the little Somersetshire village of Norton St. Philip, on the road from Warminster to Bath, is one of the earliest and most fascinating of large inns. The date of its foundation is given as 1397 and it was built for the wealthy Carthusian priory of Hinton, serving the double purpose of accommodating wayfarers and providing a centre for the weekly market and annual wool fair, which were under the priory's charge. As both its original purpose and exceptional size would indicate it was never solely a village inn and from one point of view was a sort of medieval Exchange, a large upper room being used by the wool traders. The original building was entirely of stone and of this the lower part survives, though the two upper storeys were destroyed by fire, probably in the late fifteenth century, and then replaced by the projecting half-timber storeys seen in our illustration, this historic patchwork giving an effect of informal beauty. At the back the Gothic and ecclesiastical character of the inn is even more pronounced, in the mullioned and traceried windows, the stone stair-turret and part of the original gallery, and here one has the feeling of being actually transported back to the time of Henry IV.

Cromwell and his Roundheads lodged here during the Civil War and the "George" again figures in political history during the Monmouth Rebellion, the Duke of Monmouth staying the night there in 1685 before the Battle of Sedgemoor. He appeared at one of the windows and narrowly missed being shot (presumably by one seeking the price on his head offered by James II)—though only to become a captive a few days later and to be beheaded on Tower Hill. Yet the inn's main historical interest is social rather than political, and it constitutes a truly wonderful monument of the religious and economic order of the Middle Ages.

Photo: British Travel and Holidays Association

The George Inn

The "Swan", Lavenham

A Tudor inn in a Tudor town, the "Swan" at Lavenham in Suffolk, has a picturesque dignity recalling the great period of the town's prosperity in the fifteenth and sixteenth centuries when its blue cloth had European fame and the merchants who prospered on its weaving industry built its great timbered houses, its Wool Hall and Guildhall. The inn incorporates four houses, three with records back to 1425, and the oldest parts may date from the late fourteenth century. As the centre for the packhorse trains that once brought cloth from such neighbouring weaving villages as Lindsey and Kersey, it formerly had stabling for fifty-eight horses. The first floor of its long wing was once an open gallery; in the yard is an outside door to an upper room, used probably in loading wool on the waggons waiting below; it boasts within the most authentic of low-ceilinged, beamed Tudor parlours with an open basket hearth and a maze of stairways and corridors at different and unexpected levels.

The "Swan" was so flourishing in Charles II's reign that its landlord issued his own trade token under the sign of the house; in the early eighteenth century, the first traveller's guide to Suffolk made it the measure of road distances; though with the progress of the Industrial Revolution and the decline of the region's "domestic industry" (long though it lingered) it lost the old local basis of its prosperity. One old art which continues is that of the church bell-ringers who here perform with handbells. Recent history is written in the smoke-room bar in the form of the signatures on the walls of men of the 1st Airborne Division who fought at Arnhem and of both British and American air force crews during World War II. Much beautiful timber work has been uncovered in the last quarter of a century, a fine open-hearth fireplace also, and on the Water Street side exterior there remains a trace of early moulded plaster decoration, fleur-de-lis, mitre and Tudor rose.

Photo: Trust Houses Ltd. (A. C. K. Ware)

SWAN HOTEL
TRUST HOUSE
RAC
GCF 358

The "Lygon Arms", in the famous village on the western slopes of the Cotswold Hills, has a number of claims to eminence among English inns: its long history, the beauty of its architecture—that of the sixteenth-century Cotswold stone house at its best—and also in restorations and additions so well carried out that the building has gained in total effect. It dates back to about 1530 and was then called the "White Hart", a name it retained for 300 years, until after 1815, General Edward Lygon (pronounced Lyggon), an officer at Waterloo and son of the first Earl Beauchamp of Madresfield, bought the Spring Hill estate, Broadway, and sold the inn to his steward, requesting that it should be known as the "Lygon Arms". Jacobean features are due to John Treavis, landlord from 1604 to 1641, a man of some wealth, who added the front doorway (1620) on which his name and that of his wife Ursula are carved and also the handsome plaster ceiling, frieze and stone fireplace of the room where, tradition has it, Cromwell slept before the Battle of Worcester. Some written evidence points to Charles I having met his supporters here in 1645 and a room with seventeenth-century oak panelling is known as the "Charles Room".

It was prosperous in the eighteenth century and the great coaching period, and the Honourable John Byng, who so much enjoyed its "delicious loyn of veal", could not imagine "a cleanlier, civiller inn than this is, which bears all the marks of old gentility". The decay of road travel had reduced it, however, to a poor state by 1903 when it was bought by a man of taste and enthusiasm, S. B. Russell, who not only restored (in the best sense of the word) but added a remarkable collection of Elizabethan and Jacobean furniture, perfectly in place and as choice as a museum might contain. Structural additions were made with respect for the character of the building and the region.

The story of the "Lygon Arms" would not be complete without reference to its offshoot, the Russell Workshops, in which Sir Gordon Russell, R.D.I., first began to make modern furniture in which the quality of the old craftsmanship was preserved.

Photo: British Travel and Holidays Association

The "Falcon", Stratford-on-Avon

Stratford-on-Avon, so rich in timbered Tudor buildings, offers a handsome example in the "Falcon" situated in the Shakespearian heart of the town. It would have been a familiar sight to Shakespeare in his youth and after he returned to Stratford to live in New Place (the property he bought in 1597 for £60). The "Falcon" overlooks the gardens of New Place (rebuilt in 1702 and demolished in 1759) and is close to the thirteenth-century Guild Chapel and the Grammar School where Shakespeare was educated. In his lifetime it was a private house but records show that it was an inn "called by the name Falcon" by 1640. As an inn name, "Falcon" has been traced back to the emblem of the House of York; it may also have had some general sporting association with falconry though here it possibly referred to Shakespeare's crest. Twenty-four years after Shakespeare's death, it was kept by a man of commercial substance enough to issue his own token coins, Joseph Phillips. He supplied wines to the Corporation and in 1675 was a witness to the conveyance of New Place from the trustees of Lady Bernard, Shakespeare's grand-daughter, to Sir Edward Walker. Of historical scenes it has witnessed, mention may be made of the arrival of Queen Henrietta Maria to stay at New Place with Shakespeare's daughter, Mrs. Susanna Hall, during the Civil War, when the Queen was on her way to join Charles I near Edgehill. At the "Falcon" in 1824, the Shakespeare Club, harbinger of the annual celebrations in his honour, was inaugurated.

It is strange to think that its riches of timbering were externally covered with stucco until as late as 1930 but in the decade following it was restored—or rather returned—to its pristine condition. In addition to its own plenty of massive beams, some interior walls are lined with oak panelling taken from New Place itself.

Photo: F. W. Callaby (Paul Popper Ltd.)

THE FALCON HOTEL

The "Bell", Stilton

The "Bell" at Stilton in Huntingdonshire is notable on several counts; as a fine example of the Cotswold tradition in stone building; as a famous stopping place on the Great North Road in the coaching age; as the original source of the popularity of Stilton cheese; and in addition for its imposing sign. Built in the seventeenth century, the material being a warm sandstone; it bears a certain resemblance to the "Lygon Arms" at Broadway in its dignified gables and refinement of style, though Georgian interpolations were made, like the wooden sashes replacing the original stone-mullioned windows—no doubt intended to signalize its modernity as a coaching inn. It was its sporting landlord, Cooper Thornhill (who rode a horse from Stilton to London and back, *c.* 1740, in record time), who made known to the world the nobility of the great cheese, by supplying it to his customers and, despite its coming in fact from a dairy in Leicestershire, made it Stilton's for ever.

A beautiful aspect of its sign is the highly decorative wrought iron of its bracket, though the size of the copper panel on which the bell was painted was intended to attract principal notice. It has been precisely measured as 6 feet 2¾ inches and is said to have been the source of many a wager between coachman and passengers which the former for obvious reasons invariably won. Like other great coaching inns the "Bell" declined with the progress of the railways and, sorrowfully commented Charles G. Harper in 1906, "they look at you with astonishment when you want to stay the night"; yet between that day and this the revival of the road intervenes and the "Bell" in its present aspect looks as trim and inviting as it must have done when the "York Highflyer" and the rest of the procession of coaches paused on their way, north or south.

Photo: British Travel and Holidays Association

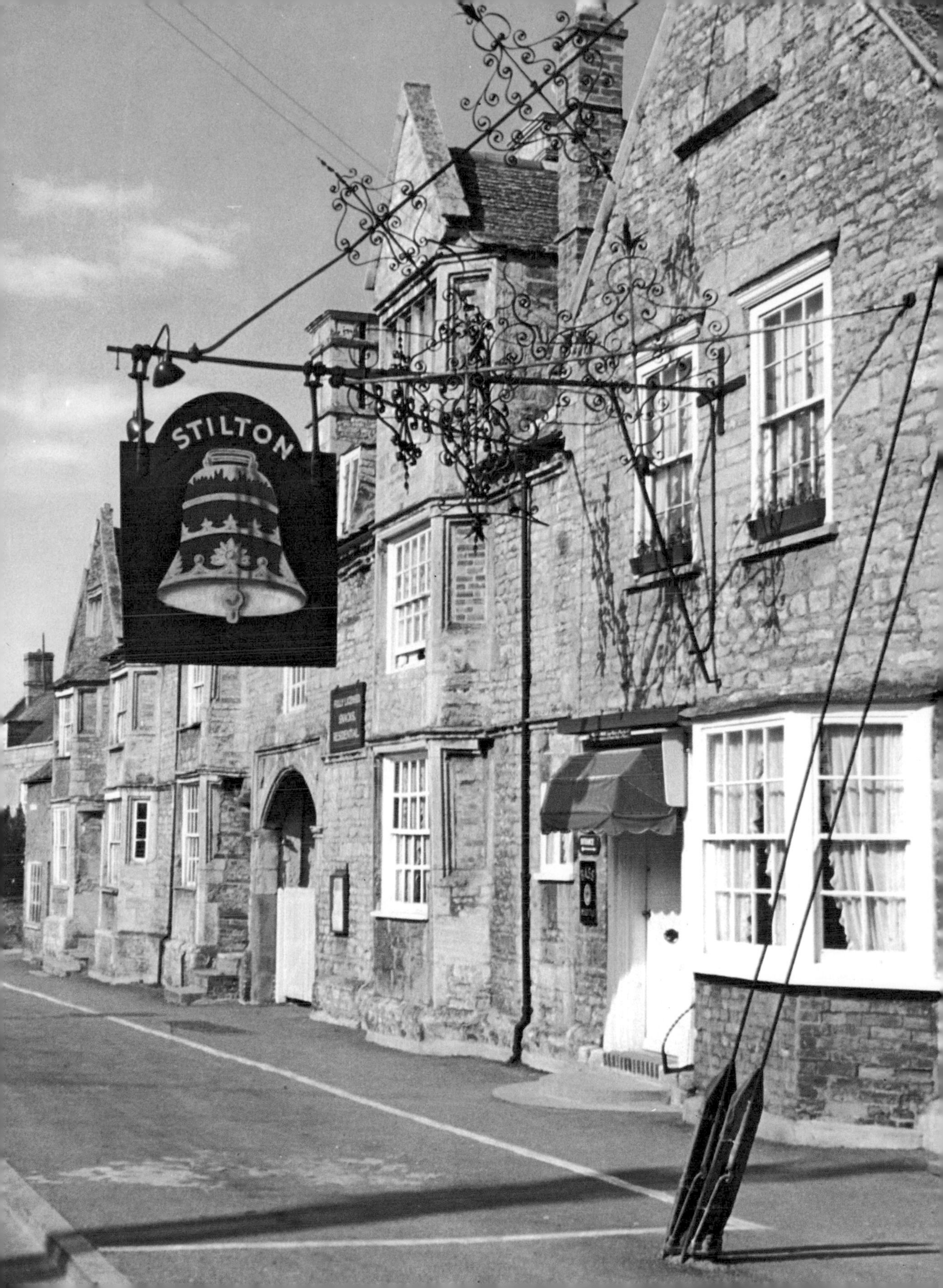
STILTON

The "Bear and Billet", Chester

Among the many sumptuous timbered houses of the sixteenth and seventeenth centuries for which the city of Chester is famed, the "Bear and Billet" inn has a distinguished place, being superbly decorative and varied in its "black-and-white" pattern of woodwork, though architecturally its long range of window glass might almost be considered "modern" in conception.

It may be compared with such other picturesque gems in the city as Bishop Lloyd's House, Leche House, the (reconstructed) God's Providence House and Tudor House. The illustration conveys the magnificence of the great single gable, the rich effect of detail and what that connoisseur of old inns, Charles G. Harper, called "its satisfactorily conservative condition".

The word "billet", derived from the Norman-French for a log of wood, and implying also a post or wooden stave is often met with in the names of old inns, and "Bear and Billet" is no doubt a variant of the Bear and Ragged Staff, the famous device of the Earls of Warwick. Yet it was a late christening, for originally this was a private mansion, the town residence of the Earls of Shrewsbury. The Talbot family, Earls of Shrewsbury, were hereditary Sergeants of the Bridge Gate adjoining. As communications with London grew easier, the need for such a town house away from the capital grew less and it was leased to an innkeeper with the provision that a suite of rooms should be perpetually reserved for the family, when their ceremonial office or other occasion made their presence in Chester necessary. The inn remained their property until 1867.

Photo: British Travel and Holidays Association.

HOME GUARD
·CLUB·
WORTHINGTON'S
ALES
ONLY
ON DRAUGHT.

The "Angel", Lacock

This inn at the Wiltshire village of Lacock, between Chippenham and Melksham, noted for the thirteenth-century remains of its abbey, quite wonderfully conveys a feeling of venerable and gracious age, to which the neighbouring buildings contribute, e.g., one sees in the background an interesting example of the old curving "cruck" beam, supporting both walls and roof of a cottage. Flagged roof, gabled front, Tudor woodwork, stone-mullioned window make up that dignified and beautiful effect typical of many old country houses in Wiltshire, their number being a marked feature of the county, anciently among the chief of the clothing counties and thence until the seventeenth century gaining much prosperity.

The name, it has been suggested dates it back to *c.* 1465, when Edward IV introduced the gold coin known as the "Angel Noble" and familiarly as the "Angel". Pre-Tudor features include the Perpendicular stone doorway and some of the original fireplaces remain. It has alternated between inn and private house and was once for a time the dwelling of a well-to-do clothier but in this century has reverted to its original function. If one leaves out of account the window casements of a later day, the scene our illustration presents has no feature later than the Tudor age.

Photo: H. J. Stapleton

ANGEL

“Ye Olde Bell”, Hurley

The mellow haze of time and legend which hangs thick about many old inns makes it difficult to be exact about their date of origin and there is perhaps a score of claimants to the title of the “oldest inn in England” whose claims cannot be decisively proved or denied. Among them is “Ye Olde Bell” at Hurley in Berkshire, five miles from Maidenhead and near the Thames, which has been said to date back to 1135 and to have been the guest house of the neighbouring Priory of Lady Place, formerly in the See of Westminster. The existence of an underground passage leading to the monastic ruins has been offered in evidence—this, more specifically, consisting of a caved-in tunnel which begins in the ruins of the Priory and is assumed to connect with a similar tunnel located beside the old fireplace of the inn. Here is a field for romantic speculation—the sign itself begins to suggest the tolling of the priory bell for matins and compline—and legend is so often well-founded that there may have been an earlier building than that we now see, though the latter may be assigned to the late fifteenth to early sixteenth-century period. Beyond any question, however, its timbered and white-washed front, projecting upper storey and varied gables are delightfully picturesque and the ground floor front has gained in attraction by the timbering revealed in comparatively recent years. A high-backed oak bench of respectable antiquity adds to its charm, while a modern sign with its suggestion of an ivy-mantled belfry is in every way appropriate.

Photo: A. F. Kersting

YE
OLDE BELL

The "Red Lion", Colchester

When Colchester was the Roman *Camulodunum*, some stately building stood on the site of the "Red Lion"—we may assume it stately on the evidence of the two Roman mosaic floors found beneath the hotel premises during excavations in 1857 and 1882. A thousand years later, some monkish or other building of the Middle Ages stood on the same spot, the cellars of the "Red Lion" revealing its medieval masonry, in which Roman tile and rubble is incorporated. By these impressive stages we come to the antiquity of the present building, built probably as a private mansion, *c.* 1470, and converted into an inn, *c.* 1500, when the main part of the street front took its present form. It was first called "Le Whyght Lyon" and did not therefore, like so many inns, directly take the *lion gules* from John of Gaunt's shield, but perhaps from the Scottish emblem, exchanging white for red, it may be, with the union of the Crowns. Restored, with admirable discretion and respect for the structure, since 1913 by the Trust Houses Company, it has many features of exceptional interest, the flamboyant tracery and grotesque heads of the wooden panels on the High Street façade; the carvings of St. George and the Dragon in the spandrels of he arched gateway to the courtyard; the splendid beams of kitchen and dining-room, part of the original Hall of the mansion before its conversion; on the first floor landing, a four-light fifteenth-century window; many details coming freshly to light as renovation went on.

The "Red Lion" was well placed as a market centre—in 1529 it was ordained that the "pease and root market, with the onions, garlick and cucumbers . . . shall be holden and kept from the Lyon Sign downward towards St. Nicholas Church and in no other place". Later it had its share of coaching business. A "stage cart" with a good tilt (covering) set out thence for London, *c.* 1756, while in 1839, the "Blue" coach, between London and Ipswich, called there every evening (Sundays excepted) at six.

Photo: Trust Houses Ltd. (*A. C. K. Ware*)

RED
HOTEL
HOUSE
WIRELESS

The "Manor House Hotel", Cullompton

Once the home of Sir John Upcott, a wealthy wool merchant, this hotel-inn, in Cullompton, the first Devonshire town to which the traveller comes from Somerset, combines features of the early seventeenth and early eighteenth centuries. The woodwork of the façade is Elizabethan and a stone panel, carved with the initials T. T. and the date 1603—the last year of Elizabeth's reign—indicates the earliest known owner of the house, one Thomas Trock. The exterior effect of the four gables and range of windows is stately and not lessened by the observable contrasts of period style.

The old manor house was renovated in 1718 and the new construction of this time accounts for the appearance of a classic element. The doorway with its double shell porch, supported by Doric pillars, is believed to have been the work of an Italian plasterer who also brought some houses at Topsham harbour near Exeter "up to date" in the same "Queen Anne" or early Georgian sense. A cistern head at the rear of the building, decorated with cupids holding a rose-wreath, bears the date 1718. As change of taste so often dictated, much of the Elizabethan oak panelling was then covered over by pitch-pine with a heavy moulding. Some of the original panelling has been uncovered in recent years. Other historic features of decoration are a fireback in the lounge bearing the royal cypher, C.R., and date, 1635, and an Adam mantelpiece and moulded ceiling. The town leat which runs directly before the hotel is part of the ancient history of Cullompton, having been the gift of the Abbot of Buckland to the townsfolk in 1285.

Photo: A. F. Kersting

THE
MANOR
HOUSE
HOTEL
QUEEN ANNE
CAFE
CAFETERIA
MANOR HOUSE HOTEL

The "New Inn", Pembridge

What may well be called a gem of the "black and white", half-timber building of which Herefordshire has so many fine examples is the "New Inn" at Pembridge, a little township also noted for a fine, half-timbered Market Hall and ancient cottages. The "New Inn" is said to have been founded in 1400, but, no doubt, as with numerous other inns of the same title, "new" indicates rebuilding and the style brings us to the flourishing period of the sixteenth century. There are a number of indications of intended decorative effect derived from structural detail, like the carved finial of the projecting upper storey, but, in addition, age has added delightful adventitious effects of irregularity in the thickness, thinness and spacing of the beams and struts which retain all the natural character of the oak—produced by the soil of this county in great plenty. The whole of the Welsh Marches and the country adjacent to the River Severn is rich in this style, and the "New Inn" at Pembridge may well be compared with the "Feathers" at Ledbury and perhaps more closely with another inn of similarly decorative aspect, the "Red Lion" at Weobley, only a few miles away from Pembridge; the two might, indeed, to judge by their appearance, be the work of the same builder and craftsmen.

Photo: E. G. Meadows

The "Lord Crewe Arms", Blanchland

This is certainly one of the most remarkable inns in England, made out of the remains of the Abbey of Blanchland, a twelfth-century foundation dissolved in 1539, though the conversion of the abbey kitchen and Prior's house (the stone-vaulted chamber of which now forms a bar) belongs to a much later date. Its aspect and story cannot be separated from that of the whole group of buildings comprised in the village of Blanchland, which in effect is an eighteenth-century model village built on the plan and from what was left of the medieval abbey. It thus gains a special distinction of appearance as if, says Mr. S. P. B. Mais, "an Oxford college had been transplanted in its entirety" to this beautiful but isolated region of the valley of the Derwent and amid the moors of Northumberland. In the seventeenth century the estate was held by the Royalist family the Forsters who used a remaining part of the abbey as a manor house. It was bought by Lord Crewe, Bishop of Durham in 1704, who left it, and part of his great wealth, to be administered by trustees, since known as the Lord Crewe Trustees. They rebuilt most of the houses from the Abbey ruins in the eighteenth century and restored the ruined choir as the parish church. The niece of the bishop's wife, Dorothy Forster, had a romantic part in the Jacobite rising of 1715, the subject of Sir Walter Besant's historical novel, *Dorothy Forster*, some scenes of which are laid in Blanchland; and she gives a name to a room in the "Lord Crewe Arms", once perhaps the Forsters' parlour, while her portrait hangs on the wall. Eighteenth-century taste in "Gothick" added such details to the ancient stone structure as battlements and ogee windows, and the dining-room is of that date but the three-feet-thick walls and the monastic fireplace in the entrance hall are as they originally were. A Priest's Hole, cunningly concealed in a wall by one of the fireplaces, is a reminder of the struggle of old loyalties, religious and political.

Photo: British Travel and Holidays Association

The "Feathers", Ledbury

The western Midlands are especially notable for their richly half-timbered inns and the market town of Ledbury, on the Malvern Hills, not far from Hereford, offers two excellent examples in the sixteenth-century "Talbot" and the companion piece—here illustrated—the "Feathers" in the High Street. It was originally an Elizabethan house to which a Jacobean top storey was added, while a seventeenth-century block to the north, formerly the manor house, was made part of the inn in Georgian times. A wing at the back was built in the Cromwellian period and the "Feathers" also possesses an assembly room built on pillars over the stable yard. A late seventeenth-century staircase leads to the two upper floors where remains of wall paintings of the type popular in Elizabethan and Jacobean times are to be seen.

The name, like that of other "Feathers", refers to the emblem of the Prince of Wales, and possibly, like that of another beautiful half-timbered inn, the "Feathers" at Ludlow in Shropshire, commemorates the investiture of Prince Charles as Prince of Wales in 1616. In the late eighteenth century it was a posting inn and remained a coaching inn until a surprisingly late date, for we are told that mail coaches were still stopping here in 1876. For two hundred years it was its special privilege also to hold a pew in the church, granted by Captain Samuel Skynner of Ledbury, of whom there is a bust in the church, in 1717. The attractiveness of its "black and white" structure with the charming departures from absolute regularity that timber—and age—give can well be appreciated in the illustration.

Photo: Trust Houses Ltd.

RAC
HOTEL
AA
HOTEL
TRUST
HOUSE

The "Bell", Wylye

The ancient connection between Church and inn, no doubt accounts for the many "Bells" to be found in all parts of England—both in the singular and in the plural form (in varying numbers up to eight). Proximity to monastery or church, whence the sound of bells constantly came, would suggest it, though in course of time it came to be used, like other inn names, as a long-accepted symbol. The "Bell" at Wylye in Wiltshire, half-way between Warminster and Salisbury, is certainly near the church, though it would be hard now to say whether it was so named in consequence or because by the time it was built "Bell" was a popular name. As a building it has no very specific recorded history, and a search through the Deeds found no reference earlier than the beginning of the nineteenth century but all the evidence of style in its stone structure and mullioned upper-floor windows entitles us to refer it to the seventeenth century, and to find points of likeness, on a modest—though charming—scale with such well-known examples as the "Lygon Arms", Broadway, and the "Bell", Stilton. It is indeed a delightful-looking small country inn, and the sign on its wrought-iron bracket, though not competing in size with that of the famous Stilton inn, makes a brave show.

Photo: J. Allan Cash

THE
BELL INN
MORNING
COFFEE
TEAS

The "Crown", Amersham

Though it has a front of plain Georgian brick on the High Street at Amersham, Buckinghamshire, the "Crown" dates back to the sixteenth century and much of the original timber work remains in both walls and ceilings, while the inn yard has its pleasant pre-Georgian picturesqueness. Of special interest in the interior are the Elizabethan wall-paintings. The arms of Queen Elizabeth, with Lion and Dragon supporters, are painted on the wall above the fireplace in the oak-timbered lounge and according to tradition commemorate her visit to Shardeloes, a mansion on the outskirts of the town. An upper room has the whole of one wall painted with scroll ornament in blue, green and yellow, within claret coloured bands, the centre of each cartouche being veined to represent marble. Other traces have been found of what may have been a complete scheme of decoration.

The "Crown" formerly contained the Court Room, where the local magistrates sat, now a bar, to which the visitor comes by way of the pillared entrance porch. It was also one of the last of the coaching inns, if one regards a three-horse omnibus as the direct descendant of the old Amersham and Wendover Stage Coach. Until 1890, this coach-bus plied daily between the "Crown" and the "Old Bell" in Holborn, twenty-six miles away, a distance now more speedily traversed by the Underground railway system, though of this present nearness to London and its bustle one would get no inkling from the placid charm our picture presents. As in many old inns the Tudor character has been preserved in the part in which it was not considered important to advertise modernity.

Photo: Trust Houses Ltd.

The "Angel", Guildford

A modern-fronted hostelry, the "Angel" in the steep main street of Guildford has a number of interesting evidences of the past. In general, the name "Angel" suggests a monastic origin or association and here there is a stone-vaulted cellar, like a crypt of three bays supported by two stone pillars, possibly dating back to the thirteenth century and by some connected with a long-vanished priory—though this is only conjecture. That it was an ancient foundation, however, is beyond doubt and its name may well have been taken from the stone angel, surmounting the cross, erected by the White Friars in 1345, in the middle of the street at a point opposite where the inn stands.

By 1527 it had passed into secular hands and a hundred years later was one of the "very faire innes" mentioned by John Taylor, the Water Poet. It was one of two ancient establishments in the main street, the other being the "Lion" (mentioned by Pepys) and both were celebrated in the coaching heyday. In the eighteenth century it was the scene of such local ceremony as the Bailiff's Feast and the £4 paid for wine on this occasion, in 1707, no doubt represented lavish festivity, though later in the century the landlord was reduced to financial distress through the excessive billeting of troops. As late as the 1840s the "Times" coach left the "Angel" daily for Charing Cross via Epsom. The interior and rear premises retain the flavour of the sixteenth and seventeenth centuries. There is fine oak panelling in the hall, which, Thomas Burke relates, an elderly uncle told him was once used as a model for a stage set, the hall in one of the scenes of *Dorothy*. The courtyard which as in so many inns has escaped modernization presents the highly picturesque aspect seen in our illustration.

Photo: Trust Houses Ltd.

Ye Angel Hotel Yard

The "Luttrell Arms", Dunster

The fifteenth-century porch of the "Luttrell Arms", with its defensive cross-slits, the quaintly gabled seventeenth-century Yarn Market and in the distance the Norman castle, acquired by the Luttrells in 1404, give a composite pictorial history of the Somersetshire village of Dunster, two miles from Minehead and the Bristol Channel. The inn grew round a Gothic Hall, built, so local history relates, by the Abbot of Cleeve, the monastery some four miles distant, and the Hall remains, though divided by a floor into two, the upper room with fine hammer-beam roof being a lounge and the lower the hotel bar (it was for many years the kitchen), while carved oak Gothic windows are a notable feature comparable with the Tudor window of the "King's Head" at Aylesbury. Apart from the porch the front has been a good deal modernized.

Originally called the "Ship", the inn changed its name in compliment to the Lord of the Manor, Hugh Luttrell, in 1499, and the martlets of the Luttrell arms are carved in stone over the entrance. A feature of considerable interest in one of the rooms is a seventeenth-century overmantel in moulded plaster, with figures in Jacobean dress, shields with the arms of France and England and a central panel depicting the Actaeon of classical legend devoured by his hounds. It seems very likely that this decorative work was carried out by Netherlandish craftsmen attracted to Dunster by its old cloth-weaving industry, of which the Yarn Market is a symbol. Another ancient feature is the skittle alley, which has been in use since the sixteenth century. As a dignified and commanding presence in a village noted for its beauty, the "Luttrell Arms" may well be compared with the "Lygon Arms" of Broadway.

Photo: A. F. Kersting

The "Old Ferry Inn", Bodinnick-by-Fowey

Perhaps some inn or tavern stood here when Fowey in south Cornwall was an important seaport of the Middle Ages where ships for the crusades were fitted out and where Edward III mustered a fleet of forty-seven vessels for the siege of Calais; the old ferry itself is reputed to have been in operation since the thirteenth century, between Fowey and Bodinnick. The "Old Ferry Inn" does not, however, claim a longer history than four hundred years and one is tempted to muse on the gatherings of Elizabethan seadogs in its stone-floored ale-house-bar which is its oldest part. It has a beautiful setting, near that deep and sheltered harbour now dotted with yachts and motor-boats, and is seen to advantage either from the descent to the ferry on the Bodinnick side, as in our illustration, or from the town of Fowey where it appears embowered between tree-clad slopes suggestive of the luxuriant foliage to be met with along the Fowey river. The inn itself has a special charm in its simplicity of architecture and its harmony with its surroundings.

Photo: K. Scowen

The
Old Ferry
Inn

The "Angel", Corbridge

Standing at the crossing of roads between London and Edinburgh and Newcastle and Carlisle, the "Angel" of the market town of Corbridge, Northumberland, has a position which has given it a long history as a coaching inn. It has been an inn since the early sixteenth century, still retaining a Tudor window. It was here that Thomas Cromwell's Commissioners stayed when negotiating with the dignitaries of Hexham Abbey, three and a half miles away. The corner stone, known locally as the Coigns or Quoins, is traditionally the point at which the people gathered to watch the arrival and departure of the stage coaches and to hear what news had been brought, and the cobble stones are worn smooth where they have always sat.

Its setting is the same beautiful country as that of another inn of unusual interest, not far away, the "Lord Crewe Arms" at the unique village of Blanchland. It is less than a mile from the Roman camp of Corstopitum, the original Corbridge, which served as base for the military operations of Antoninus Pius and where the ruins of Roman granaries were unearthed in 1907, silver dishes and gold coins having also been found on the site. It is also near Hadrian's Wall itself, that stupendous monument built in A.D. 121, and three and a half miles from Hexham and its great abbey church with its Saxon crypt and its magnificent Early English architecture, first built in A.D. 674 of stone brought from the disused and ruined Corstopitum. A Tudor inn is almost a newcomer among these monuments of a remoter past yet the "Angel" has four hundred years of history and many old architectural features in good preservation.

Photo: British Travel and Holidays Association

THE ANGEL INN
HOTEL

The "Swan", Grasmere

This Lake District inn, which dates back to the seventeenth century, is distinguished on two counts, by the grandeur of the surrounding scenery with which its plainness of exterior so becomingly harmonizes and by its association (and that of the lakes and crags around) with Wordsworth and his fellow poets of the Lake School. Helvellyn is not far away, Helm Crag is within easy climbing distance, high up the fell above the hotel to the east is the great rock, Stone Arthur, in Wordsworth's words "the last that parleys with the setting sun" while the beauty of Grasmere lake and vale needs no elaboration here.

The original sign of the "Swan" was painted by its host, Anthony Wilson, inciting Wordsworth to write—in less than his most lofty strain—the lines in "The Waggoner":

Who does not know the famous Swan,
Object uncouth and yet our boast,
For it was painted by the host,
His own conceit the figure planned,
'Twas coloured all by his own hand.

Wilson is to be numbered among famous innkeepers and was the friend of Hartley Coleridge who wrote his epitaph when he died in 1831 and was buried in Grasmere churchyard.

Sir Walter Scott when staying in the region certainly used the "Swan" for, as the story goes, when he and Wordsworth paused at the inn in 1805 on their way to climb Helvellyn (to view the scene of a mountain tragedy which inspired both to a poem) the innkeeper greeted him with the remark, "Why, sir, you've coom seun for your glass today." Thus he inadvertently made the abstemious Wordsworth aware of regular visits he would not perhaps have viewed with favour. One needs however no literary association to appreciate the natural beauty of the "Swan's" setting and the appropriateness of its architecture which a number of additions to the original building have not made less.

Photo: British Travel and Holidays Association

The "Dolphin and Anchor", Chichester

The double name of many old inns often points to the amalgamation of two at some stage of their history and this is so with the "Dolphin and Anchor", formerly adjoining hostelries which in the eighteenth century were rivals not only for custom but in political views, the "Dolphin" being a Whig and the "Anchor" a Tory house. It stands in the centre of the medieval city, close to the great cathedral and fine (Perpendicular) market cross, and in what was also the centre of the Roman city *Regnum*, and, it may be fairly assumed, on the site of Roman buildings, though of them no trace remains even in the ancient and extensive cellars. The oldest part of the existing building is roughly dated by a stone built into one of its chimneys marked 1519. By 1660 the "Dolphin" was an important posting inn and in 1672 the Corporation entertained the Lord Lieutenant of Sussex here, the house then being the largest in the city after the Bishop's palace. Always prosperous, and therefore constantly altered and "improved", it presents to the street a sober late-Georgian front typical of the coaching era and as an old guide-book says, "not without a certain dignity befitting an episcopal city", only one small part of an earlier frontage being left. Another feature of its later growth is the Assembly Room, said to have been built for Whig meetings by John Abel Smith, M.P. for Chichester, while old sporting prints and furniture are eloquent of Regency days. The diarist Thomas Creevey, who stayed here in 1828, gave the "Dolphin" superlative praise, and in the Victorian age it remained well cared for by its owners, the Ballards —a family of local note—one of them being Posting Master to the Queen. A Mrs. Ballard who died in 1874 was distinguished as the last person in Chichester to use a sedan chair.

Though "Dolphin" may ultimately derive from the French "Dauphin" there is perhaps no need to see in the name more than a suitably marine symbol (like the associated "Anchor") for an inn not far from the sea and on the main road from Portsmouth and the West to Brighton.

Photo: Trust Houses Ltd.

DOLPHIN HOTEL

The "Pleasure Boat", Hickling

The name presents none of the mystery which so often sets us guessing about origin and historic significance; it could not be either more obvious or apt. The "Pleasure Boat"—here it is, delightfully placed among the shallow lakes and waterways of the Broads and among pleasure boats, which provide it, as it were, with a series of mobile and floating signs. This is not one of those inns whose development we trace from century to century in remarkable features of architecture and their connection with great changes in methods of transport. The same type of boat has always glided quietly past that delightful garden and mooring-place, though no doubt as the Broads grew more frequented, the little house by the water became in the most easy and unobtrusive of ways a place offering hospitality. It is rather like a natural feature of the region than an hotel purposefully set down there; its charm lies in its homely simplicity.

By its position, however, in this region of open-air sports and pastimes, it has its special distinction among the "inns of sport". "No inn in the whole of Broadland", observes J. Wentworth Day in his *Inns of Sport*, "has seen more skating or ice-hockey than the 'Pleasure Boat' at Hickling. There, indeed, is an inn of all sports. Pike-fishers gather there with duck-shooters, the mighty men of Hickling Cricket Club, the crack clay-pigeon shots of the Hickling Gun Club, and once a year in winter all the men of gunpowder who come from far and near to take part in the famous Hickling coot shoot. . . ." Our picture, however, conveys an idyllic quality, suggestive of summer ease and quiet exploration of the watery world which is the "Pleasure Boat's" unique estate.

Photo: G. Douglas Bolton

THE
PLEASURE
BOAT
TELEPHONE

The "Hoops Inn", Horns Cross

Thatched inns are not confined to one English county but Devonshire has many examples and one of the most attractive is the "Hoops" at Horns Cross, half-way between Clovelly and Bideford and a mile from the sea. "Hoop" as the name for an inn may have some distant connection with the circle of leaves which formed the original "bush" sign but in the plural more readily suggests the hoops of a barrel and perhaps may refer to the bands at equal intervals round a quart pot. It is credited with a very ancient history, though one cannot be explicit as to date; is linked by legend with the old smuggling days of North Devon and was later a coaching inn, particularly reputed, it is said, for its home-brewed ale. A "museum piece" kept here is the "Lorna Doone" coach which saw service in the last century and even in the early years of this century drove between Minehead and Lynton.

Architecturally it is not the outward sign of great age but a trim simplicity that appeals to the eye, the neatness of thatch, the clean white walls, the black-painted woodwork—from this point of view its attraction is timeless. The thatched porches are an addition of recent years.

Photo: K. Scowen

HOOPS
INN
HOOPS
INN

The "White Hart", Witley

This pleasant detail of the tile-hung porch and front of the "White Hart" at Witley in Surrey shows its considerable architectural charm, and one notices incidentally the present version of the celebrated sign painted by Birket Foster and Alfred Cooper in 1875. According to local legend there was a building here, erected at some time in the late fourteenth century by Richard II as a hunting lodge. The Manor House adjoining the premises, a royal residence, was at that time assigned to one of his retainers, but Richard, it is supposed, did not wish to forgo the pleasures of hunting in the district. It is not easy, however, to relate the "White Hart's" evolution as a building with historic legend, though the inn proper, as distinct from the added hotel buildings, has old features. Its history seems to be obscure until the beginning of the eighteenth century, and it was then, during its ownership by an old West Surrey family, the Lunns, that it received its licence and sign. The white hart badge of Richard II was adopted as an emblem by many old inns, but local legend here made it especially apt. In the nineteenth century it did duty as a village alehouse but the growth of motor traffic in our own day made enlargements necessary in which the whole was welded into a building still characteristic of the Surrey countryside.

Photo: K. Scowen

The "Sportsman's Inn", Cowgill, Dentdale

An equation is easy to make between sport and the English inn, seeing that both are so much bound up with the English tradition—as Mr. Wentworth Day has observed, "Every sport deserves its good inn and, in truth, most good inns are homes of sport." Certainly there are many with some special sporting association. They include the old inns of the racing fraternity, like the "Turf" at Doncaster where Lord George Bentinck for a while stabled his entire stud, or the "Rutland Arms" at Newmarket, hunting inns like the "Bull" at Rolvenden in Kent, or the "Sun" at Ruthwaite where the hunting horn of John Peel is preserved, inns popular with duck-shooters in East Anglia and angling inns in every part of the land. It might be adduced as extra proof of a necessary connection between inns and sport that they are often decorated by racing, hunting and coaching prints or by stuffed fish in glass cases. The "Sportsman's Inn" at Cowgill proclaims its happy union of traditions and its special function as simply and clearly as the "Pleasure Boat" of Hickling, though viewed pictorially it is no less sympathetic to the landscape of the region than to the sports there carried on. In aspect it seems timeless, one is scarcely concerned to date it, though one knows it is old, it belongs by its character to its region and is in perfect union with the trees, rocks and streams of the Yorkshire Dale country.

Photo: G. Douglas Bolton

The "New Inn", Clovelly

The high street of the fishing village of Clovelly on the north coast of Devon, situated in a cleft of the rocks, goes steeply down four hundred feet to the sea and this situation gives a special charm to its little whitewashed buildings, among them the "New Inn". It may be compared with the "Old Ferry" at Bodinnick-by-Fowey in Cornwall which has a not dissimilar sloping site. Pictorially, they make a delightful pair, both being set amid magnificent scenery and in fascinating relation to open water.

The "New Inn" retains an old simplicity despite rebuilding, *c.* 1920; broken only by one of those little balconies which the nature of the site seems to suggest as a counterpoise to the steep descent; is perfectly in place and no more elaborate effect is necessary than the flash of whitewashed walls against the colour of the sea. It has been said that the "New Inn" might call for little remark if it stood by itself on a main road, but in its local setting, of which it is a harmonious part —and touched by the coastal magic—it takes on beauty, and few inns have more often set the open-air painter to work or been more often photographed.

Photo: K. Scowen

The "Black Swan", Helmsley

An ancient inn of the North Riding of Yorkshire, on the edge of the moors, the "Black Swan" at Helmsley is the sturdy growth of four centuries. Vestiges of the house that was standing when in former days the pack horses laden with wool came in from the moors to Helmsley, the chief market town of Ryedale, are stone walls, nearly three feet thick, oak ceiling timbers dressed with the adze and a great open hearth (uncovered within the last quarter-century), though the front speaks of the late Georgian age when the "Black Swan" as a flourishing posting and coaching inn was externally brought up to date. Some old features, not of the original structure but none the less of interest, are the Jacobean panelling in the hall which came from the parish church when it was rebuilt in the 1860s, the stone Tudor doorway leading to the cellar, assumed to have come from the sixteenth-century wing of Helmsley Castle, and a rockery made of stone from the castle walls. In recent times the inn has extended to take in the Georgian house next to it and the latter's stylistically contrasting neighbour.

As the head inn of the town the "Black Swan" was the setting for such occasions as Jury Dinners and the Annual Rent Dinner of the Duncombe Estate tenants, while a traditional part of its fare is venison from the deer park of Lord Feversham's seat, Duncombe. It is also an appropriate rendezvous for the local hunt, as our picture conveys, the Sinnington Foxhounds meeting there regularly. Rowlandson would have delighted in the scene thus presented, though he would not have failed to delight also in the natural setting and the magnificent ruin of Rievaulx Abbey, no more than three miles away.

Photo: Trust Houses Ltd

THE
HOTEL
TRUST HOUSE

The "First and Last Inn", Sennen

An interesting list could be made of the geographical and topographical names of inns. There is the comprehensive "Globe"; the humorous comment on Captain Cook's discovery of Australia, "The World Upside Down"; that curious evocation of crusade and pilgrimage, the "Trip to Jerusalem" (suggestive not of tripping in the modern sense but of a halt on the way) and, as striking as any, the "First and Last", though this is not the philosophic generalization it might seem but has precise reference to local topography. The inn so named at Sennen, in Cornwall, a mile from the cliffs of Land's End, thus indicates that it is the last you come to —or the first—according to direction. Land's End itself produced rival "First and Lasts", but the inn at Sennen claims to have been the original begetter of the name.

In appearance it retains a strongly local character, harmonizing well with the grey granite church by which it stands, and leading one perhaps to recall the time when this westernmost point of the country, terminating in granite cliffs and roaring seas, was a wild and lonely region and the inn a solitary haven—in the days before "touring brought civilization". Its simplicity makes an emphatic contrast with the elaborate old inns of town and highroad but has a quality of its own.

Photo: Paul Popper Ltd.

The "Langton Arms", Tarrant Monkton

It is an impressive thought that there are some seventy thousand inns and ale-houses in England, that in pursuit of them research leads not only into the cities and towns and along main roads but off the beaten track, along winding lanes and to cloistered and peaceful villages where the small inns, distinct in kind from the larger hostelries, typical of their locality and so much a part of local life, are to be found. Their modesty of aspect and of interior furnishing is part of their charm, they merge into the attractive picture made by the straggling village street, the varied pitch of roofs of thatch and tile. Inside they will have that plainness that George Morland loved and painted, though if often later than Georgian, they are still traditionally rural and a tall wooden settle or a much used shove-halfpenny board speak of their local and club-like character.

In the agricultural county of Dorset at the village of Tarrant Monkton (with a population of some 212) we come to such an inn essentially of the village scene, homely and, with its little garden, hardly to be distinguished from the other cottages though its bright heraldic sign proclaims its function. The sign is not a fanciful addition of heraldry but evidence of that link with the social structure of the region which has so often bestowed the arms of the principal landowner and local family on an inn. The "Langton Arms" was so called when the Farquharson family bought all their Dorset property, round about 1750. They themselves lived at Langton House, Langton, near Blandford, and allowed their own coat of arms to be thus used. Here is an interesting example of the extent to which heraldry and social tradition have coloured inn signs and names.

Photo: K. Scowen

FIDE ET FORTITUDINE

The "Crown and Anchor", Dell Quay

There are little inns on the coast or close to it—in an entirely different category from the hotels of the seaside resorts—which derive a special charm from their setting, and the "Crown and Anchor" at Dell Quay in West Sussex, near Chichester, is one such, so attractively is it placed by a creek and in relation to boats and shingle. Though it has something of the look of a private house, it was built as an inn and its history is said to go back much longer than its façade might suggest—more than four hundred years. It is one of its traditions that there should always be a light as a landmark in the window facing the harbour and this still continues. Like other coastward inns of Sussex and Kent, counties to which the smugglers of the early nineteenth century could most easily deliver their French brandy and lace, it has also its smuggling tradition and the story is told of a fight in its cellars between smugglers and excisemen in which, it is recorded (without disapproval), the excisemen had the worst of it. Old games have a long life in these secluded inns, though the pastime called "Ring the Bull" apparently makes its last stand in this part of the world at the "Crown and Anchor", having at one time been popular in some half-dozen establishments round about. The picture of a bull's head hangs on the wall with a hook in its nose, a heavy ring is suspended by a cord from the ceiling, the object of the game is to link the ring on to the hook, a feat which is held to be by no means as simple as it sounds. The name of the inn, not uncommon, adds to the patriotic symbol of the crown a marine touch here obviously in place.

Photo: K. Scowen